Chaos
to
Serenity

Martha Crikelair Wohlford

Serenity
Press

To Kim!

enjoy! Marty Wohlford

Other Books by Martha Wohlford

Fiction
Drumbeat No Lie

Non-Fiction
If I Can't Be Dead, How Can I Live?

For Children
Little Star's Big Day
Splash - the Staniel Cay Cat

Chaos
to
Serenity

Stories of Staniel Cay

Serenity
Press

Chaos to Serenity
Copyright © 2009 by Martha C. Wohlford

Published by Serenity Press.

Cover art by Bernadette Chamberlain
Photography by Martha C. Wohlford

For information regarding permissions, email marty@mwpr.com.

ISBN 13: 978-0-9787981-4-7
ISBN 10: 0-9787981-4-7

Printed November 2009 in the U.S.A.

For my mother, Addie Crikelair, who loved the island...
especially the fishing.

Keeper of the Stories

After almost 40 years with close ties to the little island of Staniel Cay, midway in the Exumas southeast of Nassau, Bahamas, I've been encouraged to share the many stories that have evolved over the years. Some of them are personal. Some have been told to me. Some are amusing. Some are sad. They add up to a rich, wonderful life in a tiny corner of the world where the sun sets into the sea, boating is a way of life and people escape the drudgery of civilization.

We discovered Staniel Cay while cruising on our sailboat in the late 1960s, and quickly became friends with the owners of the Staniel Cay Yacht Club, Bob Chamberlain and Joe Hocher, who discussed the difficulty of communications and bringing tourism to the island.

After years as a charter yacht captain and marine surveyor, my husband's dream was to be a commercial airline pilot. At the time, Staniel Cay had a marginal gravel airstrip about 1,200 feet long, mostly used by Sandy Malcolm, who built several of the early homes on the island. He and Harold Hartman, another American, built the new runway in the early 1970s so that Harold and his family could safely fly to their vacation home. By the time the 3,000-foot strip was completed, we were licensed as a charter airline. We operated TransMar International until 1986, beginning with a five-place Aztec and ending with two King Airs. As a writer and photographer with my own public relations and advertising firm, I helped put Staniel Cay on the map.

Since there was no reliable phone service to the island until 1988, we operated the airline, reservations for the yacht club, parts and purchasing for residents and cruising yachts, and provided communication via commercial single sideband radio, a simple, yet sophisticated system. If we pushed a button on our radio in Fort Lauderdale, a siren sounded at the yacht club. If they pushed a button, we got a signal that the island was calling. In this manner every type of information was conveyed 24/7: births, deaths, parts orders, messages to families...at one time I had to call two home owners to tell them their homes had been wiped out by a water spout turned tornado as it came ashore. We were the link for everyone and everything to and from the island.

Calling it the "good old days" doesn't convey the thrill of making things happen in this tiny, thriving environment.

Today the island is considered the jewel of the Bahamas. The yacht club is operated by the next generation, and in 2004, I demolished my little vacation cottage called Serenity, and built a new round house and guest cottage for my active retirement.

My novel, *Drumbeat No Lie*, is a fictional caper that takes place on the island in the early 1980s. *Chaos to Serenity* tells of real people, situations and events, It is a collection of personal experiences and memories, not in chronological order, and not only of the island. Others may have their own "take" on some of the stories, but this is the nature of storytelling. I apologize in advance if my brain cells, tinged by the warm tropical sun, play their own tune. The drums still beat, and we reggae on.

While the stories are true, some names are changed or only the first names are used. The island is a microcosm of the universe: life in miniature, yet real proportions, a constant reminder that even in Paradise, no one escapes their share of tribulations.

***

My own personal stories and experiences follow a brief history of Staniel Cay and the last section features Staniel Cay trivia. Hopefully, it will help the reader better understand and visualize the island – and maybe inspire a treasure hunt of their own.

Part 1
Staniel Cay History

A Brief Look Back

Most of this chapter is the result of hours of interviewing Capt. Burke Smith and Vivian Rolle in an attempt to begin documenting the island's rich oral history. More will be written at a later time, but for now, this gives the reader an idea of what island life was like in the early years.

Many visitors are often surprised to find Staniel Cay noted as "Staniard Cay" on some marine charts. How and when it became known as Staniel is a mystery to everyone. One theory is that it may have been confused with Staniard Creek on Andros in the mailboat system, but that can't be confirmed. For years it was known as Gray Cay, after its founder.

The actual history of the island dates back before Columbus landed, but for our purposes, history begins with William Welshcomb Gray, who, according to legend, left England by boat and arrived at Long Island in the early to mid 1800s. He eventually became the caretaker of Sampson Cay, and his employer at the time, a Mr. Miller, rewarded him with funds to purchase his own land following William's marriage to his daughter.

He originally looked at Big Sampson, but found a better anchorage at Staniel Cay, where he purchased approximately 62 acres which comprises the greater village area. William and his wife had five daughters and one son, Malchesedech, who married Georgiana Edgecomb of Scrub Hill, Long Island. They had five daughters: Agnes, Edith, Manna, Cassie and Rose, and two sons: Richard and Cleophus. Richard married Blanche Smith of Farmers Cay in Nassau in 1917, and they returned to live on Staniel Cay, while his brother moved to Nassau. Most of today's families on the island are descended from Richard and his sisters, and over the years, more surnames were added: Smith, Rolle, Cooper, Ferguson, Miller, Kelly, as husbands chose to live on Staniel Cay.

The library was the original William Gray homestead, which survived the deadly 1926 hurricane. Unlike the other tiny homes built of wood, it is a prime example of early "rubble" construction, which featured extremely thick, solid walls.

"They would tote conch shells, put them on a wood pile and let it burn down to make lime for cement," explained Burke. "They mixed it with local rocks to build the walls."

The original Rev. Joseph Miller house.

The original house built by Rev. Joseph Miller, now deteriorating off a small village path, shows this construction.

Vivian recalls that Rev. Miller's wife, Aurelia Miller from Farmer's Cay, was the first school teacher.

"School was in the little church when I was growing up," she said. "It was a Grant in Aid school, which is what all schools were called back then. We went for two hours a day, from ten until noon, and we studied reading, writing and arithmetic. School started at age five or six and went until we were fourteen or fifteen. Then we left school to help farm and survive, as we didn't have high school then."

After Aurelia passed, her granddaughter, Vanrea Rolle, returned to the island after her mother died in Nassau to care for her father, Tim Rolle. Since she had been well educated in Nassau, the government granted her permission to teach at Staniel Cay.

"At that time, in 1961, the school was moved to a small building which eventually housed the Happy People generator as my daddy, Rev. Alpheus Rolle, started building the new church," said Vivian. "Vanrea's boyfriend, Frank Minus, came with her and never left."

The church built by Rev. Kelly in 1961, also used as the school.

Staniel Cay's All-Age School.

After a few years, Vanrea's drinking became a problem, and the government asked if there was someone from the community who could replace her as teacher.

"Creighton Thompson, daddy's nephew, grew up in Nassau and was educated there. He applied for the job and became our first 'real' teacher. That's when the school curriculum changed. It was in session from nine to three each day except Friday, when there was a half day, with history, literature, religion and other subjects added."

Subsequent teachers have improved the quality of education, and the island now has a dedicated school house. In 2009, there were sixteen children with two teachers, including two of my grandsons.

***

Life in those early days revolved around farming and fishing. Besides beets, cabbage, corn, carrots and potatoes, the island also grew sisal and cotton for export to Nassau.

"The community farm was on the site south of the cemetery and included where the teacher's house, playground, clinic and old Chamberlain lot are today," she said. "We also farmed South Staniel, which was separate back then. We either waded across the creek at low tide or sculled a little boat at high tide."

Each family also had fields on Sampson Cay, Big Majors Spot and Bell Island, growing pidgeon peas, potato and Guinea corn. With the advent of the freight boat bringing food from Nassau, farming gradually stopped as tourism changed the island economy. Burke Smith was the last one to farm off island, which he did until the early 1990s.

Burke also talked about the sponge trade, which was prevalent until a blight killed all the sponges in the Bahamas.

"Back in 1945 to 1950, me and my dad went sponging on the south side of the Exumas. We'd leave early in the morning and sometimes wouldn't reach until sundown, depending on the wind," he said. "We'd look over the side with a glass bottom bucket and hook wool sponge, grass sponge, reef sponge. The wool sponge was the strong one."

He said they would put them on a line, let them dry, then put the dead sponges in sea water to soak them clean.

"The stench was bad," he said, wrinkling his nose. "Our little boat was 13 feet and our big boat was 17 feet. We'd live and sleep aboard sometimes spending three, four weeks at a time, hooking over a hundred sponges a day. Then we'd sail them to Nassau where a merchant would buy them for export to the States. You didn't make much money as a sponger."

He said in those days, the creek between the airport runway and the ocean ridge, now dredged for larger boats, was so shallow they could walk across and pick up hundreds of conch.

"Then we'd sail them to Cat Island or Eleuthera where

we'd trade for peas and corn. Conch was like our money."

Burke also recalls the sisal trade, where families on Staniel Cay would cut open the sisal plant, lay the fibers along the ground, tie them together, then string them out in the creek to soak with the tides.

"The sisal would sink to the bottom at first, but after a week or two when it was finished washing, we'd lay the fibers on a tree to let them dry, then ship them to Nassau," he said. "We'd 'bail the sisal,' packing and trimming each box so it was two-by-three-by-two feet. It was a lot of labor."

He also talked about fishing, when every variety was plentiful throughout the islands.

"We would leave Staniel Cay about two in the morning, and when the day was clean (sunrise) we would be south of Duck Cay, almost to the end of the Exumas. Then we'd cross to the Ragged Islands. We'd get grouper, turbit, margate, yellow tails, but mostly grouper and turbit as they lasted longer in the live wells. After four or five days fishing the Raggeds, we'd head to Nassau. Sometimes it would take twenty-four hours, depending on the wind. We'd go to the fish market, where they'd pay us a dollar or two for a grouper, then we'd buy flour and rice. Today that same fish would sell for $70 to $80. It was a struggle to support the family back then."

The start of tourism in the early 1970s was the turning point for the island.

"People would bring stuff for us...the Arteagas, the Wohlfords," he said. "It made a big difference."

Today there is no unemployment on the island. If someone wants to work, they can, with good wages and plenty of opportunity. There is ongoing construction and development in the area, but tourism continues to be the main industry.

The Staniel Cay Yacht Club

It is by chance that Staniel Cay has a world-class marina and resort.

Burke Smith explained that years ago, a group of Nassau businessmen who loved to sail, decided to put fuel drums on an island midway between Nassau and Georgetown for their own convenience. John Maura, founder of Maura's Lumber in Nassau, originally dropped the fuel drums at Black Point, but was told the community didn't want them there. He moved them to Staniel Cay where the yacht club now stands. There was deep water, it was convenient, and the community welcomed him.

"He leased the spot from Gray and put in a pump so they could hand-pump fuel into their boats on their way to Georgetown for exploring the cays," said Burke. "Then in 1959 Mr. Maura said he wanted to build a yacht club. When he started, I was his right-hand man to do all the masonry work for the new underground fuel tank. It was built where the deck is at the club."

Bob Chamberlain was one of the first partners, along with Roy Arteaga and Sydney Heig out of Nassau. A little log cabin for their own lodging was built where the fourth cottage now sits.

"The first club had a thatched roof, two little bathrooms and kitchen. After he opened the club, my brother, Capt. Huey Smith, and Kenneth Rolle managed it," said Burke. "The original kitchen was where the gift shop is now, and the generator was where the phone booth is. It was all very small."

Maura wanted to expand the club, but the others weren't in agreement, so Bob Chamberlain bought them out, and Joe Hocher, who arrived on a small power boat from Chicago, became his only partner a few years later.

Joe Smith recalls meeting Joe at Nassau Yacht Haven before he came to the island.

"We began to talk, and he asked me if I knew what time the mailboat goes to Exumas. I told him tomorrow. We walked out on the dock and he showed me his little plywood boat with two dive tanks, two small gas tanks for the 90 hp outboard and some clothes. He was living on it. I asked him where he came from. When he said Chicago, I thought he was crazy. I told him I was leaving at midnight and he asked if I could pull him across the banks. I told him I was going straight to Staniel Cay, so could tow him all the way. We arrived and I pointed him to the yacht club. He was here from that day on."

The club attracted a collection of yacht burgees from around the world, souvenirs of past visitors, along with boat name plates, old nautical instruments and impressive fish mounts. One of the items that became a conversation point was a parking meter cemented into the entrance garden. It eventually corroded, and when my niece cut her hand on it one night while the kids were playing flashlight

Staniel Cay Yacht Club parking meter (not a big revenue producer).

tag, it was removed.

The yacht club is now owned and operated by second-generation David Hocher.

Happy People Marina

With the deaths of Kenneth and Theaziel Rolle, Happy People is no longer open on a regular basis. Hopefully this will change in the future and it will again thrive as a favorite place to hang out, enjoy good food and music.

Happy People dock in the 1980s.

The village in the 1980s.

Part 2
Author's History

No Go and Wind Chime

In April 1967 I willingly embarked on a honeymoon adventure with Trey, my new husband. We took a 15-foot runabout with a 70 horsepower engine called *No Go* from Alexandria, Virginia, to Fort Lauderdale. He told me it was going to be like a river. We had no compass and no charts, until meeting a flabbergasted marine at the Quantico base on our first night out. He gave us a little more knowledge and insight into our impending trip than I wanted to hear.

We left with a set of old charts to cross the lower Chesapeake to Norfolk. After shimming up pilings at low tide and pointing to our little boat when the dock master asked where we came from, he introduced us to some people on a fancy sport fish that had returned to the dock after finding the seas too rough. They looked at our little red boat bobbing below and asked, "Who's your psychiatrist?" I won't go into the details of that first trip down the inland waterway except to say it was a once-in-a-lifetime, great experience.

A couple of weeks later we arrived in the Venice of America, assuming we could find a place to dock *No Go*. We pulled into every marina off the Intracoastal in Fort Lauderdale, and

Marty, Trey and the No Go *in Appleton, Wisconsin*

none would have us. We were too small. No revenue. In desperation, we tied up to a little abandoned dock just off Las Olas Boulevard and A1A across from the charter boats. A large multi-storied condo is there now.

We used the bathroom at a gas station across the street, and enjoyed the beach every day. Then we met a couple by the name of Walt and Judy from Michigan who were also on their honeymoon, who had wanted to do the trip we had done, but were discouraged by their family. They had a rented apartment and we had the boat. Combining our resources meant a good time. We took advantage of anything free to do, including a plane ride to the west coast of Florida, sitting through the swamp land sales pitch and a quick tour of some developer's dream on paper. When they found out neither we nor our friends had any money, they ignored us and pumped the other happy tourists with their dreams of sunshine living.

We did get a good view of the Florida Everglades, which from the air, looked as if the earth had gotten sick, with the swirl of water mixed with the yellows of sawgrass and palmetto trees, dark creeks probably filled with alligators meandering midst spots of higher green hammocks.

When it was time to head back to Wisconsin, we bought a boat trailer and Walt and Judy agreed to drive us back to the midwest as we'd bumped enough on the way down the waterway. Back in Appleton, we settled into our routine. I was women's editor of a small local newspaper, and Trey ran one of the family's women's clothing stores. Four months after we were married we had no merchandise in the store due to a series of local disasters (street being redone, dust in the store, fire in a store next to ours that sent smoke through the vents to ours, etc.), so we packed up my Triumph TR3 two-seater sports car and headed south via Kansas to visit Trey's favorite aunt. It was like driving in a blast furnace with no air conditioning in August.

With a few saved and donated dollars, we managed to buy our first sailboat in Fort Lauderdale, an already aged 36-foot Alden design sloop, from three guys who had just sailed the Bahamas, who left a bilge full of unidentified canned goods. No one told us the consequences of a stick (mast) that went to heaven and a keel (six-feet!) that went to hell. It was NOT

Wind Chime *in Fort Lauderdale*

a southern cruising vessel. But it was home. What did we know?

In order to help with expenses, we invited a couple from Wisconsin to join us for a week in the Florida keys. They would pay all expenses and we'd supply the boat. Soon after they arrived, we realized they were expecting a conventional charter vessel complete to stocked bar and galley, with cook, steward, mate and captain in the likes of me and my husband.

Off Elliott Cay near Miami, our poor choice of boat became painfully clear. We ran hopelessly aground. No matter the gorgeous view of the original "stiltsville" homes on Key Biscayne, or of clear blue waters winding into the little harbor. Our guests couldn't appreciate the scenery and thought the situation wretched as they tried to sit upright in *Wind Chime's* heeling cockpit.

A sympathetic boater gave us a tow to Miami's old Fifth Street Marina where upscale Bayside now attracts international visitors to its trendy shops, funky kiosks and world cuisine food court. It was the commercial fishing docks in the late 1960s, a rundown, grubby mixture of smells, missing dock planks and not-so-yachty boats. Our guests hopped a cab and were gone. We had no money, a broken starter motor, and my husband had no shoes. He'd left them in Fort Lauderdale, not thinking he'd need them. It reminded me of our trip on the *No Go*, when Trey refused to pack long pants even though it was early April. We had to purchase some in Elizabeth City, North Carolina.

Yes, we were young and foolish, and we desperately needed $100 to get the starter fixed to get back to Fort Lauderdale.

So, I got out my guitar and started singing on the docks

for whatever anyone would throw in the hat. It wasn't the tourist meca it is now, and we figured it would be awhile before we got back to Fort Lauderdale.

Then we met Manny, a husky Bahamian from Bimini with the most wonderful smile and laughing eyes who, as a young boy, had baited hooks for Ernest Hemmingway. He had heard about our situation and asked if I could type. I told him yes, but I didn't have a typewriter. He said he'd find one, and if I typed a letter for him, he'd pay me $50, the fee a secretarial service was going to charge him.

By the next day, his letter was in the mail. Years later, I realized what an important letter that was – to Lynden O. Pindling, Esq., a lawyer who became the first black Prime Minster when the Bahamas achieved independence in 1973. Years later I would dance with Pindling at Happy People in Staniel Cay during the New Year's Annual Cruising Regatta celebration.

***

We had just gotten jobs and had *Wind Chime* tied to a nice dock on the Isle of Venice, where in exchange for dockage we maintained the pool and lawn, when Trey's dad suddenly died of a heart attack on Oct. 31, 1967.

It took all our money to get back to Wisconsin for the funeral and we knew it would be some time before we would have enough money to return south.

We put the boat up for sale in the shipyard where Trey was working, and gave ourselves a year to make some money, buy a better boat, and return.

Wind Chime took longer to sell than we thought, competing with newer fiberglass sailboats, so in February, we took two weeks to do a quick trip to the Bahamas. Another couple came with us. Again, we were young and foolish.

Marty and Trey aboard Wind Chime

With only a two-week window, we crossed the Gulf Stream in a northeaster, arriving in Bimini in the dead of night with our unforgiving deep keel that could have been ripped off had the gods not threaded our way through the jagged reef. We dropped anchor and passed out from fatigue. Our guests had been no help, stayed below decks the entire crossing, and were totally terrified.

The next morning, I poked my head out of the companionway and fell in love. I had never seen such exquisite water, all shades of aqua starting with deep blue just offshore, to transparent where the sea met the white sand beaches. There was that particular salty smell of the sea mingled with whisps of pungent sea life and humanity. I have never forgotten that magical moment when the Bahamas claimed me forever.

As we threaded our way to the old Weech's dock to clear customs, a familiar face stared down at us with the biggest smile in the world. Manny! He dragged us off the boat to Brown's for breakfast, explaining he'd deal with the custom's officer himself.

Unfortunately, our guests didn't catch the magic and took the first available Chalks seaplane flight back to the States. We explored the Bimini chain, snorkeling the relic concrete ship, anchoring in Honeymoon Harbor, and then reluctantly sailed back to Fort Lauderdale with friendly winds. The boat eventually sold, and we spent a year working in Wisconsin saving money, dreaming and planning our return to boating and Florida.

We subscribed to every yachting and sailing publication. Weekends we traveled to Door County in Wisconsin, where Palmer Johnson builds beautiful new boats and where marinas were full of yachts, or to the Lake Michigan coast where there were many marinas and boats for sale. One thing was certain: our next sailboat would have a shallow draft and would easily be handled by two people.

The first week back in Fort Lauderdale in late 1968, we found *Toko Maru*, a comfortable, 35-foot Allied Seabreeze yawl, with a shallow draft ideal for cruising the islands. She had everything we required and was also in our price range. We found jobs and docked *Toko* up the river near State Road 84 to get the lowest possible dockage rate. We spent many hours giving *Toko* lots of TLC.

We soon advertised her for bareboat charter, and with our first booking, bought linens and cookware.

When the first charter party discovered we had nowhere to go for that Christmas week, they invited us to join them. Oh Lordy, what a week! I remember it as super party time, with bottles accidentally dropped overboard retrieved by their friend named Woody. We were asked to leave one marina, ran out of fuel between islands, and generally went in circles while primarily partying. It must have been a good week because we remained friends with Fred and Barbie over the years. He eventually was appointed a federal judge in New York. Barbie, widowed, visited me at Staniel Cay in 2007. We are forever friends.

The first year we had *Toko*, I worked as a feature writer under Edee Greene, executive women's editor of the then *Fort Lauderdale News*, now *Sun-Sentinel*, and Trey worked on boats, building a reputation as a competent captain of both sailing and motor vessels.

We eventually sailed *Toko* to Nassau, basing her for bareboat charter out of Coral Harbor on the west side of New Providence. Every week a charter ended, Trey would fly to Nassau, collect the previous week's laundry, put the clean linens aboard, greet the next charter group, check them out, and fly back.

I can still see those big army-green seabags full of sheets and towels that I took to the laundromat, as we still didn't

Toko Maru *under sail off Fort Lauderdale.*

own a washer and dryer.

One of Trey's favorite stories took place while hitchhiking from the airport to the boat to save cab fair, lugging all the clean linens. A car full of maids headed for work in the secluded homes of Coral Harbor picked him up, everyone in a good mood. Trey got joking around with them and said he was curious about all the stories of Bahamian men boasting about their "inside" as well as "outside" children.

He asked the women how they felt about all those "outside" children, and they all laughed. One said, "Well, all dem inside chillen ain't all inside."

Just when we were starting to get ahead in the bareboat charter business, the gasoline engine died. We sailed *Toko* back from Nassau with the help of Capt. Chuck Willard of *Mata Hari*, a 62-foot custom sloop that Trey often sailed on as first mate. Off Bimini, the mainsail headplate wore through and the sail dropped. Trey hoisted Chuck up the mast in the bosun's chair while I tried to keep the boat steady in a rolling

Mata Hari, *left, and* Toko Maru *at anchor in the Bahamas.*

sea. Chuck was over one side, then the other, until he finally was able to reach the fitting. We somehow rigged the mainsail and limped back to Fort Lauderdale.

With no money to put in a new, more efficient, diesel engine, Trey went to the bank for a loan. The bank asked for collateral. Trey offered the boat. The bank said without an engine the boat was worthless. We were dead in the water. Then the phone began ringing. Within three days we had enough charter deposits on the way to pay for the new engine. Once again, our prayers were answered. Surely God has a sense of humor.

***

In November of 1969, before putting *Toko* back to work for the season, we decided to enjoy her ourselves and take a couple of months off to cruise the Bahamas.

I approached my boss and told her our plans. I asked for the time off with the idea of doing feature stories along the way for the newspaper. She took the plan to the higher ups who flatly said, "No." She told me I'd probably start having kids and would never have the chance again, so, with a mischievous twinkle in her eye and a big smile, she advised me to quit, saying she'd try to find a position for me when I returned.

Trey believed in all the creature comforts, so before we embarked on our cruise, he made sure we had a cruising generator to run an ice box that he had converted to an electric refrigerator with a holding plate to make ice cubes. In today's age, this is no big deal. Back then, it meant designing and fabricating the box for the plates, and experimenting with various solutions for the right anti-freeze and water combination to get the temperature of a deep freeze. Comfort also meant towing a 13-foot Boston Whaler, complete to a set of water skis, for going ashore, snorkeling, and having fun. Today it is commonplace. In the late 1960s people cruised with no refrigeration and tiny little rowing dinghies for going ashore, many willing to trade their first-born to swirl their rum in a glass of ice cubes.

The week before we were to leave for the Bahamas, we had to brake on State Road 84 in Fort Lauderdale to avoid hitting a small black dog. We stopped to make sure he was all right, and discovered he could hardly walk for all the cockleburs and twigs tangled in his poodle type matted hair. He had a collar, so we took him to our apartment, which did not allow pets, and tried to find the owner. After numerous calls to no avail, someone at animal control asked us if we liked the dog.

We said, "Yes, he's adorable, friendly and happy to be with us."

The man replied. "You've now got a dog."

Trey and I contemplated this helpless, pathetic looking animal looking into our eyes and knew that we did, in fact, now have a dog. We cut all the burrs out of his hair, bought dog food and told him we hoped he liked sailing because he was going to sea in a few days.

We soon discovered that the dog was extremely "male friendly" to anyone and everything, and hence, decided to call him "Friendly," not realizing that his behavior would never change. He was, indeed, a friendly dog.

The day we started our cruise down the New River heading for Port Everglades and the ocean, a small boat made a huge wake passing us and Friendly, who had taken his position as figurehead on the bow, with ears flapping in the breeze and his nose in the air, went overboard in downtown Fort Lauderdale. I looked up to see the huge tour boat *Paddlewheel Queen* bearing down on us as it wound its way to its secret island up river, where passengers would disembark on a short plank to see authentic Seminole Indian alligator wrestling while enjoying the usual hot dog/hamburger fair in the "wilderness of Old Florida." The boat schedule was so routine you could tell time by the bridge openings twice a day.

As Trey got the Boston Whaler ready to rescue the dog, frantically paddling toward the boat, I put *Toko* crosswise in the channel, forcing the *Paddlewheel Queen* to start her second engine and move toward the seawall.

We yelled, "Man overboard!"

The captain was not at all happy when he discovered our "man" was a dog, but there were cheers from everyone onboard as Friendly was pulled dripping wet from the river.

We headed south out of Port Everglades to ride the Gulf Stream and did the usual route: Bimini, where we cleared Bahamas customs and visited our friend Manny, across the banks to Chub Cay, into Nassau. After grocery shopping, which also included a few bottles of rum, we headed for the Exumas, which to this day, is considered some of the best cruising in the world.

At Allan's Cay we watched conchs on the move in the shallow seagrass beds, propelled by putting their foot out and dragging the shell a little at a time. We didn't see the iquanas, but we did see the remnants of a shipwreck, old timbers buried in the sand.

At Norman's Cay, we took the Boston Whaler back into the pond, exploring and looking for shells while Friendly enjoyed some shore time. Trey accidentally stepped on a conch shell buried in the sand, giving him a puncture wound. We headed back to *Toko* and sailed to Staniel Cay where we met Terry and Dolly aboard *Different Drummer*. Trey's foot was hurting, and Terry and Dolly gave him some antibiotics they had onboard.

We left Staniel Cay and sailed to Black Point, where we spent a couple of days (story follows). We headed to Farmer's Cay, and anchored in the little lagoon off the cut to Exuma Sound. I was reading *Wind from the Carolinas* by Robert

Toko Maru *under sail in the Bahamas.*

Wilder, and realized we were anchored right where that part of the book took place.

Trey was now running a high fever, his foot was extremely painful, and we became concerned because there was no medical help until we reached Georgetown.

By the next morning it was critical he see a doctor, so we got underway. Terry and Dolly were also on their way to

Georgetown, and I was able to reach them on the radio and tell them our plans and predicament.

I don't know how I got the boat to Georgetown. We didn't carry a lot of fuel, so we had to rely primarily on the sails. Trey was able to help put the them up, but by the time we got to Georgetown he was delirious in the bunk. I managed to get the sails down and motor to the Georgetown dock, where Terry and Dolly were waiting to help. It took four men to lift Trey out of the boat and into a jeep someone offered.

It was a Saturday morning, so we took him to the doctor's home, which was highly unusual in those days. The doctor, from South Africa, at first did not want to treat him, but he eventually agreed, explaining what he had to do and that he didn't have anything for the pain. I told him to do whatever he had to do, and we all held Trey as he cut into his foot to relieve the pressure, clean the wound and bandage it.

He was able to give him more antibiotics, and Trey was again carried back to *Toko* where, thank God, he soon began feeling human again.

There was a community picnic the next day, but when I saw the doctor and approached him to say thank you, he turned away. Today he would accept a big hug, but not back then.

After a few days, Trey was ready to sail again, and we headed south, bound for Rum Cay. At that time, very few boats ventured that far south. As we were anchoring, Friendly, always the opportunist, suddenly leaped off the boat, swam ashore and began running along the long sandy beach toward the village. We quickly got in the Whaler to chase after him.

As we pulled up to the small dock we were greeted by someone asking if we were looking for a little black dog.

We said, "Yes!" and the man smiled.

"I 'spect he knowed all de lady dog by now," he said. "He shor quick about it."

I believe Friendly changed the lineage of all future dogs on Rum Cay, and he certainly gave us an unusual welcome to the island.

We soon met an American who was living on Rum Cay who had a small airplane. He and Trey started talking planes and flying, and we were invited to fly to Long Island with him, where he had to pick up a package. I regret to say that he tossed a beer can out of the plane before taking off in the little four-seater. At that time I was afraid of flying in small airplanes (I eventually conquered that fear when I got my pilot's license in 1978) and was happy when we arrived back safely. I've just never gotten over the realization that I climbed into a plane with a man I had never met, who was drunk by midmorning. I'll chalk it up to again being young and foolish.

Because we were only the twelfth boat that anyone could remember anchoring at Rum Cay that year, and it was already December, the lobster had little knowledge of humans. Trey jumped off the boat with mask, snorkel and fins, went down about twelve feet, and got one of the biggest "bugs" I have ever seen in all these years in the Bahamas. He held the feelers with the tail almost touching the ground. It became several meals.

Since there was little protection from the wind and seas at Rum Cay and bad weather was predicted, we headed to Long Island where there was better anchorage. Along the way, the seas began to build and the wind whipped to almost gale strength. Trey was at the helm and I held Friendly in my lap in the cockpit. The poor little dog couldn't stop shaking, and

I have to admit I felt the same way, as we almost broached several times when the sea hit broadside, spilling over in a froth as it swept under us.

Trey asked me to turn around and check to see if the Boston Whaler was still in tow. We had put a very long tow line on because of the seas. I told him I could NOT look back. Then we saw the Whaler in FRONT of *Toko*. The sea had swung the boat around and we had a near miss avoiding our own tender!

We finally got into smooth waters as we came around the point of Long Island, and thankfully anchored. We stayed near Stella Maris for a couple of days just to overcome that rough sailing and to put things back in order that had tumbled out of lockers and off the bunks.

Next stop was Cat Island, then Little San Salvador, where the gorgeous pink sand horseshoe shaped beach was full of tiny dead sand dollars. I gathered as many as I could, storing them in a box layered with tissues. They became Christmas presents for family and friends after coating them with fiberglass. This beach later became a favorite stop for the huge cruise ships from Nassau bound for points further south, and I was sad to realize it would never again be the wild and pristine place of our visit.

We eventually made it back through Nassau to Fort Lauderdale without any more catastrophes. We docked *Toko* and were planning to drive to Wisconsin for a family Christmas. There was an urgent message waiting from Edee Greene, my old boss. I called and she said a position was open for me starting the first of the year.

She had an "I told you so" tone to her voice and I could feel her smiling. I was thrilled!

***

One story I wrote while on that cruise was about Black Point, a community five miles south of Staniel Cay where, to this day, there is little tourism.

I'm including it because it describes the community as it was at that time.

Black Point, Exuma, 1969

This settlement, about five nautical miles south of the popular yachting stop of Staniel Cay, is a Bahamian community that is almost self-sufficient with the exception of flour and rice, which comes by freight boat along with other goods ordered from Nassau.

Situated on a rather large bay, the natives rely mainly on the good fishing grounds. Every day when the tide is right, the smacks, with their baggy sails, sail off the anchor to catch the island's evening meal. It is the man's job to catch, the children's job to clean, and the women's job to prepare.

Life here is quite simple, and rather beautiful. According to the *Yachtsmen's Guide to the Bahamas*, Black Point settlement is the largest in the Exuma Cays, with the exception of those on Great Exuma, with a population of about 300 adults and "innumerable children."

Yachtsmen rarely stop here on their way to points further south, so when we did, we received a warm welcome.

As we set our anchors, we could see the children swimming in a little cove, playing with miniature sailboats they had made.

One of the first things we have to do when we arrive at any island is take our little dog, Friendly, ashore, and when we did, the children didn't quite know how to take him. Island dogs throughout the Bahamas all seem to look alike, called potcakes, so a poodle variety is viewed with skepticism. When they discovered he wouldn't bite and that is name was Friendly, he soon ruled the roost on the island, with all the kids taking turns walking and petting him.

There are few motor boats as fuel is expensive, so all of the children wanted a ride in our Boston Whaler. We took as many as possible – 18 at one time in a 13-foot boat!

Later on it was the children's pleasure to show us their island – all "innumerable" of them, all trying to hold our hands. Their bare feet were like so many tom-tom beats on the paved sidewalk that runs through the settlement.

Cars and motorbikes are nonexistent. The children explained the "big people" keep the walk swept.

One of the first things they showed us was their school, definitely the nicest building on the island. When we asked them if they liked school, there was a chorus of "Yes, Mam. Yes, Sir."

The school gives them a primary education, but children have to go to Nassau for further schooling.

The homes, little stores and bars are characteristic of native construction, very small, but colorful. Green, pink, blue, yellow – they dot the hard rock on which they're built.

There is a telecommunications center at Black Point, which enables the islanders to keep in contact with the rest of the islands. A nurse staffs a government clinic, and the island commissioner keeps an office here.

In the evening, a couple of native men sculled out to see us, and we invited them aboard. Although fishing is the main occupation here, one had been a migrant laborer in the States for eight years, going as far north as Wisconsin to pick fruit. He couldn't get over how "cheap" things were in the United States. He had nothing but good comments on the way he was treated. The other man works at a development on another nearby island.

When we walked through the settlement, we saw corn, peas and potatoes growing. The children talked about grapes, guavas, mangos and papaya. We also saw a pen of chickens.

One of the fisherman named Emanuel invited us to his home to see his bananas. This doesn't sound like it would be too exciting, but when you see the hard rock and feel the pride the Bahamian has in growing his crops, it is really something to see.

The banana tree was in a hole in the rock

which was about five feet deep. Emanuel explained the reason for this "pothole" planting: it's the only place where there is soil. His coconut tree was planted in another hole. He had just cut a bunch of bananas off the tree and had it in his cook house to ripen.

One thing interesting about the Bahamian home: the natives cook and eat in one structure, and sleep in another. The cook house is like an old fashion cellar – dark, cool, with no furnishings. It's a rare house in a settlement to have a dining room.

In the evening we watched the native women going to the well for water, balancing pails on their heads as they walked back to their home. Even though Black Point has no running water, it is lucky to have fresh water wells, hard to find in the Bahamas, and which are kept protected.

Two native boys offered to take Trey fishing in the morning. Since it's not a woman's place to fish, I stayed on board *Toko* while they went to get our evening meal, which turned out to be crawfish (lobster).

It was difficult to say goodbye to these friendly people, so we just casually set to leave. One man on shore noticed and hurriedly sculled out to us – with a bag of peppers for seasoning fish.

The Wreck of the Toko Maru

Written in 1971

At 1 a.m., Dec. 24, 1971, I climbed aboard *Toko Maru* as the seas crashed over her. I took the sterling silver racing plaque that has been on the sliding hatch for more than five years, and struggled through the debris to unbolt a photograph taken at anchor at sunset in Honeymoon Harbor during a cruise.

I was ready to go home.

"You know," my husband, Trey, said, "She even looks beautiful on the beach."

We sat and watched the northeast wind pluck the halyards against the mast. The tide was rising, but *Toko*, firm in the sand, ignored each wave that seemed to punctuate her fate.

A yacht on a beach is defenseless, crippled. It's a sight that stirs remorse even in the non-sailor.

Her crew abandoned her, frightened, wet, cold. Her anchors couldn't hold in the heavy sea on the windward shore. So she gave up, heading alone over a rock shelf and onto Delray Beach, Florida, her rigging and sails intact. Her port side stoved in, the inside looking like a stick of dynamite had gone off. Later, it took five days to find all the parts

Toko Maru off Delray Beach, FL, Dec. 24, 1971.

to the coffeepot – sand, salt water, the ever-wicked northeast wind had won another battle against man.

***

Who was the crew that night on the *Toko Maru*? A bareboat charter party. A group of sailors off for a fun two weeks in the Bahamas. This incident, like others, shows what a problem it is in screening charter parties. The captain had credentials, but somewhere along the line, he underestimated the power of the sea, his own sailing ability, and how to control a panicked crew.

We will never know exactly what happened, but this we

Toko's *galley is unrecognizable.*

do know – *Toko*, just out of the yard, had her diesel engine overhauled, new batteries installed, new life preservers, fire extinguisher, bilge pump and life harnesses before leaving Fort Lauderdale four days before the incident. She was outfitted for her fourth season – everything was in top order.

What happened then? Speculation can go on forever. But basically, it comes down to the qualifications of the charter party, not only in boat operation, but handling their guests and making sound, often quick decisions in an emergency.

Toko being dragged to deep water and Miami for restoration.

Toko *restored and ready to launch.*

***

On Jan. 5, 1972, *Toko Maru* received her freedom. Although patched and with bilge pumps running, she was towed back to sea.

Now in the process of being completely restored, she has again regained her dignity. Soon she will be as fine a yacht as the day on which she was originally launched.

But her bareboat days are over. From now on she'll only sail on a skippered basis, confident her pride will not again be ruined. Our "lady of the street" is about to launch a new career.

***

Since we could no longer get insurance as a bareboat, Trey docked *Toko* across from where we honeymooned on the *No Go*, and for the next year or so, he took tourists out day sailing. If the weather was too rough on the ocean, he'd tack

Trey and our sign at Las Olas and Seabreeze Blvd., Ft. Lauderdale.

along the Intracoastal or in Port Everglades, or motor up the river for a tour of downtown Fort Lauderdale. He also scheduled a few week-long captained charters in the Bahamas.

I always stayed in Fort Lauderdale, scheduling the boat, running my public relations business, and taking care of our first baby, John, born in October 1971.

We dreamed of one more family cruise aboard *Toko* before she returned to Fort Lauderdale.

Staniel Cay was as far as Trey would sail in a week from Nassau, so he spent time on the island, getting to know Bob and Joe, as well as many local Bahamians. He would come home with wonderful stories about people he had met, the possibility of doing business with the yacht club that would help everyone, and, of course, stories about catching lobster, snorkeling the wonderful reefs and coral heads, fixing dinner for six guests on a really small boat, etc. He slept in the cockpit or on deck during these charters, because there were only six bunks aboard *Toko*. Today's charter guests would never hire that small a boat with captain, but back then, there weren't as many choices as now. It was always an adventure.

While most guests were easygoing, Trey had one group that soured him forever. They were demanding, arrogant, obnoxious, did not appreciate anything he showed them no matter how beautiful, and treated him like a servant. It was the "last straw."

Our final cruise was about to begin.

The Staniel Cay Express

In July 1972, I got a very garbled, crackling message from Trey on the old ship-to-shore radio where the operator had patched him through to the telephone in Fort Lauderdale. All I remember is that he had kicked the charter party off, that he no longer wanted to do charters, and if I wanted to sail on *Toko* one more time I had better get to the Exumas the next day. I was to fly to Nassau, go to the Potter's Cay docks, walk over to City Market to buy rum and any groceries I wanted,

Marty holding John on the Stanel Cay Express rail, Nassau.

get aboard the *Staniel Cay Express*, which was to sail at eleven o'clock the next morning, and he would meet me at Sampson Cay, where he was anchored with the boat. He had made special arrangements with Capt. Rolly Gray to stop at Sampson Cay on his way to Staniel Cay.

Today it would be no problem. In 1972, a year before the Bahamas gained independence from Great Britain and Lynden O. Pindling became the first black prime minister, the natives were restless in Nassau.

At the time, my 14-year old sister, Lisa, was visiting in Fort Lauderdale, helping me with John, who was only nine months old. She thought it was great that she'd get to go to the Bahamas. I had only hours to make flight arrangements, get money together, pack clothes as well as food and formula for the baby.

After a sleepless night, we were at the airport by 7 a.m. for the first flight to Nassau. I had only flown to Nassau a few times before but had never arranged a taxi, etc. by myself. I sensed hostility and didn't feel safe from the moment I arrived, even with John in a carrier on my back.

We got our bags into a taxi, I told my sister to not say a word, and we were eventually dropped at Potter's Cay dock, where we found the aging *Staniel Cay Express*. I talked with Capt. Rolly Gray and he said I should go to the store myself and leave my sister with the baby. He gave me directions and said he would watch over them.

I remember almost running to City Market, avoiding the stares and ignoring the comments from young black men along the way. I bought as many groceries as I could carry, including a huge bottle of rum, and hurried back to the boat as I didn't want to miss sailing time. They were still loading.

At 1 p.m. they were still loading. At 3 p.m. they were still loading. On Rolly's advice, I walked to Kentucky Fried Chicken for a bucket of goodies to sustain us for the trip, again with anxiety over being a young white woman by herself in troubled Nassau.

By 5 p.m. the *Staniel Cay Express* was fully loaded, complete to a vehicle strapped to the front deck. There were other passengers, mostly natives returning home, and we were assigned various small cabins. There was little deck space other than the bow, with a small companionway outside the cabins, which took up most of the room on the vessel.

It turns out there were two more white people: a man who lived on the island and a pilot for Eastern Airlines who was going back to his boat at Staniel Cay. They both appeared drunk. To my disgust, we were all put in the same cabin, as if being white made us close family.

Let me describe this "cabin." There were four bunks, top and bottom, that measured about two feet wide by five feet long on either side of a two foot wide separation. We were given two bunks on one side for me, my sister and John. It was physically impossible for all three of us to sleep in those tiny bunks, so my sister and I took turns standing and tending the baby, who was used to a crib, not a regular bed. I barely had enough head room to stand up. The pilot had to bend over, as he stood about six feet, definitely taller than the cabin ceiling.

It was noisy. Not only did the engine pound away underneath us, but our two bunkmates continued to drink and tell stories. Using the head (toilet) on the vessel was a trip. When I needed to warm a bottle for John, I took it to Capt. Rolly, who put it near the hot engine until it was warm. I remember the captain as very friendly, helpful and understanding of my situation. He told me he knew and liked my husband, that I should look forward to a good time in the Exumas and to not mind the two men in my cabin, that he knew them to be all right guys.

What wasn't right was the boat ride. The seas had been increasing every hour we were delayed at Potter's Cay dock, and by the time we were on the shallow banks headed for the Exumas, there was a good chop and the wind was steadily blowing, punctuated by gusts every few minutes.

As the boat bounced along, another sound was added to the pounding of the engine. Women and children in the other cabins began wailing something fierce, a high pitch sound of Doomsday proportions. Most Bahamians never learn to swim, so they are terrified of the water and possibly drowning. This was loud and clear from the sounds wafting past our little two-foot wide cabin door. Capt. Rolly just kept heading for Staniel Cay, mostly ignoring the passengers and paying attention to the helm.

After a few hours at sea, I smelled food. When I opened the door, I saw native peas and rice mixed with sea water heading overboard via the scuppers. I don't know if it was before or after the meal, because there were quite a few seasick bodies onboard. I closed the door, was glad we'd bought Kentucky Fried and that all the stomachs in our cabin were weathering the sea conditions.

I went to Capt. Rolly and asked when we'd be at Sampson Cay. It was already about one in the morning and I figured we should almost be there. He informed me that, because of the late start and sea conditions, he would NOT be stopping at Sampson Cay, that he was going straight to the government dock at Staniel Cay.

While Trey knew a lot of people and spent time on Staniel Cay, I had only been there on our sailboat cruise before we had John. I didn't know a soul who could help me in the middle of the night.

About three o'clock in the morning, we docked at Staniel Cay. We and our bags were unloaded along with everything else bound for the island: sacks of wheat and rice, propane tanks, cases of beer and soda and all the other necessities for surviving on an island. It was windy, salt spray was blowing in my face, I had been up for over twenty four hours and I was exhausted. I sat down on our bags and began to cry. My sister was beside herself, and Johnny was a little angel, sleepily taking in all the commotion.

At that point, our bunkmate, Lorie, said we could go to his house, which was around the south side of the island, and wait for my husband to bring the boat when there was daylight and he could see where he was going. He said not to worry, joking that they wouldn't attack us, and to load the boat, pointing to a 13-foot Boston Whaler bobbing alongside. There was no choice but to go with the two men, who had become quite congenial (and sympathetic) during the rough crossing from Nassau.

The ride from the government dock around the south end of the island was extremely wet, with the short, choppy seas spraying deluges of sea water after slapping the sides of the flat-bottomed skiff. We were soaked by the time we got close to the beach in front of his house.

At that point, we heard another boat behind us, with someone shouting. Trey pulled alongside in OUR 13-foot Whaler, being run by a native boy. Were we glad to see him!

We loaded all our stuff, thanked Lorie and the pilot, and headed back around the south side of the island to the village.

Seeing the *Staniel Cay Express* pass by and not being able to raise the captain on the radio, Trey motored *Toko* from Sampson Cay to Staniel Cay in total darkness. There were no stars or moon out that night, and how he maneuvered around the rocks we'll never know, but he made it. When he arrived at the dock, the *Staniel Cay Express* was already gone and on her way further south. There were a few natives still picking up their freight, and he asked if anyone had seen a "white woman and a baby." One 12-year old said yes, and that he knew where we were going. For the first time ever, Trey let a native run the Whaler. That young man was Donnie, nicknamed "Yellow Mon." To this day, we still talk about the night he rescued me.

Back onboard *Toko*, Lisa and Johnny fell asleep and Trey and I opened a bottle of rum. We talked until I couldn't stay awake any longer, but that night, we sadly decided to sell *Toko*. We weren't in the financial position to keep her and our lives were taking a new direction. We would enjoy the Exumas, showing Lisa our favorite gunkholes, Trey would drop us in Nassau for a flight to Fort Lauderdale, and he would get someone to help sail *Toko* back. I'm still sad thinking about that night which ended a dream.

But *Toko* was still ours and we wanted to make the most of our last cruise, visiting Trey's favorite places on the way back to Nassau. After wandering through Pipe Creek and anchoring a couple of nights, we motored into Compass Cay, which was then owned by Herman Wenzel. Jerry and Charlotte McClish were caretaking the island and building a small houseboat to put on the two little islands in front of Compass

Bathing John at high tide on Compass Cay's dinghy dock.

Cay Harbor, called "His and Hers." We helped pound a few nails and saw plywood. It was very small, approximately eight by sixteen feet, with an area for cooking, a closet, head with shower and living area with a built-in couch and two chairs. Next to the couch was a ladder to the next level, where there was a built-in bed (no head room for standing) and an outside deck.

The Compass Cay dinghy dock, which is still there, was below water at high tide, and that's where I bathed Johnny and let him play in the water. The nurse sharks had not yet made Compass Cay their home.

When I returned about a year later, the houseboat was high and dry and Jerry and Charlotte were enjoying their hideaway along with their two little white dogs. Their dinghy dock is still there 35 years later.

McClish's houseboat on His and Hers, Compass Cay.

Jerry and Charlotte could be a separate book. His water-color paintings and instructional art books are known world-wide, and Charlotte is an accomplished potter. Today Tucker has an original McClish at Compass Cay, and I have several at Serenity. He designed the copper fireplace in what is now the Compass Cay lodge and added many personal, artistic touches when it was the Wenzel home.

After Jerry and Charlotte left the Exumas, the houseboat sat on His and Hers weathering away. The Staniel Cay Yacht Club eventually purchased it, and someone by the name of CJ (for Catamaran Joe), who built his own catamaran and sailed these waters in the 1980s, moved the houseboat from His and Hers to Staniel Cay. He liked to work in the nude, so passersby would see him hammering away in the altogether as he readied the houseboat for transport. I believe it was put on a small barge, as it was never seaworthy, and then blocked up

The houseboat cottage at SCYC.

at the yacht club as a cottage. It was a profitable venture for many years, but eventually rotted away. A new two-story cottage now stands in its place.

Incidentally, CJ was a terrific chef and also made interesting straw baskets and little creatures, fish, insects and birds out of palm tops, or thatch. The last I heard from him many years ago, he was driving a beer truck between Miami and Key West.

Back to our last cruise on *Toko*. We took our time cruising to Nassau. My sister enjoyed the many beaches, we snorkeled and shelled, and Johnny loved sitting in the back carrier that we rigged in the cockpit.

John in his back carrier aboard Toko.

When Trey arrived back in the States, *Toko Maru* was put up for sale and she eventually sold. I was so bummed I have little recollection of even saying goodbye to her, but with the proceeds, we were able to build a new house in Plantation. A portrait of *Toko Maru* under sail hangs in Serenity foyer.

***

Jerry McClish died in March 2008 at the age of 86, and Charlotte requested I scatter his ashes in front of His and Hers beach, so he could forever enjoy the beautiful view off Compass Cay. Some members of my family joined me in bidding Jerry farewell.

Sailing & New Year's Day Regatta

I can't remember if I raced the very first Staniel Cay New Year's Day Cruising Regatta in 1975, the year my daughter Coral was born, but I definitely made a point of participating in every one that I could. In 2007, I was presented the Schlacter Trophy at the awards ceremony after racing my own *Searene* for the first time. The trophy was normally given to the boat that participated in the most races, but that year, it was given to me for having crewed on various boats the most years. My five grandchildren watched me accept the trophy, which meant more to me than receiving it.

My history with sailing goes back to when I was ten years old in Neenah, Wisconsin, where I lived about a block away from Riverside Park where the Fox River bends before entering Lake Winnebago. That is where members of the Neenah Nodaway Yacht Club (NNYC), in existence since 1864 and making it one of the oldest yacht clubs in the country, anchor their sailboats every summer, the first usually launched right after the ice disappears. Opening their website, there was a message: "Cheerful news for the winter! There are only 156 days, 18 hours until the harbor opens for the season." Once you're hooked on sailing, that's it.

***

Neither of my parents liked anything to do with the water, but for me, it was a magnet, like the moon pulling me with unseen tides. Realizing the only way I was going to be able to sail as often as I liked and race in every race was to have my own boat, I pestered my father until he relented. He bought me the oldest boat in the area for $100 when I was twelve years old. It was a classic Cub X, 16 feet long, with a mainsail, jib and centerboard. She was dumped off a trailer, which was not included, in our front yard with gaping seams, torn canvas covered deck, and she was not pretty. But she was MINE. I named her *Criket*, and proceeded to learn the art of caulking. I read everything I could and talked the ear off the old salts at the club. The spaces between the planks were so large I had to use cording mixed with some kind of tar-like goo to fill them. I also peeled off the old canvas deck and stretched new fabric over the wood, then sealed it and painted it. I was determined to race.

Each year when it was time to launch, we would roll *Criket* on a dolly to the docks at Riverside Park. She would promptly sink as her caulking and old wood flooring absorbed and swelled with the river. I'd let her sit for a few days, then pump her out. She'd be relatively dry for the season, although I always had to keep an eye on the caulking. Most of the other kids, the boys especially, made fun of my boat with its old yellowed canvas sails. They had new boats, some of them made of fiberglass, with colorful decks and new white, crisp synthetic sails.

When the race committee needed one more boat for a round-robin competition for the boys one year, they reluctantly accepted *Criket*, figuring every skipper had to race every boat, so the playing field was level. When all the hotshot teens finished the competition, no one ever said anything

Criket *under sail in Neenah, Wisconsin.*

bad about my boat again. *Criket* finished overall in the middle of the pack. She wasn't the "dog" everyone thought she was, but it still didn't stop them from tossing me in the drink every time I won.

***

As a freshman at Marquette University, I made the varsity sailing team and the first year of college was spent racing, not studying. I remember driving all night to New Orleans to sail in a regatta at Tulane University during Mardi Gras. At least I THINK I remember! I know I had resentment against the guys on the team when they made me race the first race of the day because they were hung over. Duh! My head wasn't any better.

When I returned sophomore year, the university disbanded the sailing club because no one had a grade point to be an officer. Mid-year I transferred to St. Mary's College, Notre Dame, where my parents had wanted me to go in the first place, and majored in creative writing rather than journalism. One of the first things I did was walk across the road to Notre Dame to see if I could sail their boats. Members of the sailing team shooed me away. I had beaten them in every race the previous year. Thus ended my collegiate sailing days.

***

The summer I was 19, I competed on the local level for the Adams Cup, the National Women's Sailing Championship, and won the chance to sail the state championship at Lake Geneva, where we raced the new Buddy Melges design M-16 scows. It was one of his first high tech designs with vangs, outhaul, special fittings and bilge boards, and it was FAST. My crew and I won that competition and went on to the semi-finals at the Detroit Yacht Club, where I raced my first keel boat. It was like sailing a bathtub compared to the M-16 scows, but my light air experience helped us place third in the competition. I still have my trophy.

During two college summers, I taught sailing and racing tactics to kids at the NNYC, using *Criket* as one of the trainers. Today the Cub X is still a popular boat for beginning sailors and racers, particularly in the Midwest for kids up to 16 years of age. Melges Performance Yachts in Wisconsin makes the new ones out of fiberglass. Harry "Buddy" Melges Jr. is the only sailor to have won a bronze and gold medal in the Olympics and was also an America's Cup winner. He is known around the world as the greatest sailor in the sport.

***

In 1970, when I was a feature writer for the *Fort Lauderdale News* (now *Sun-Sentinel*), I complained that the sports department was not giving enough press to sailing, particularly the Southern Ocean Racing Association (SORC) races. My wonderful editor, Edee Greene, knowing how much I loved to sail, decided it was time the Living Section did a feature on women and sailing. She told me to join the crew on the boat I raced every weekend for the St. Petersburg to Fort Lauderdale race.

There were almost 100 boats entered that year. My light air experience helped as we ghosted past other boats toward the Gulf of Mexico, but by that night, the wind started to howl and it never stopped. More than thirty boats never finished the race. Some were dismasted, blew out their sails, or ventured too close to shore in almost zero visibility (way before GPS technology!) I was the only woman in our crew of eight aboard *Quest*, a 36-foot Columbia sloop, which included my husband, Trey, and Capt. Chuck Willard, who is mentioned several times in this book.

By the second day I was seasick, something I had never experienced before. I couldn't even keep down a teaspoon of tea. The seas were so rough all our food got mixed together in the ice box, which had the looks and smell of being seasick, and the whole boat was a mess. Drawers kept popping out, gear was tossed from one side to the other each time we tacked, and it was wet and miserable topsides and below decks. The stress on the hull was so great that water literally leaked in where the deck joined the topsides. I dented my underwater camera as I was flung in the cockpit trying to get photos in heavy seas. The roller furling handle went overboard, so we couldn't even shorten sail. We finished the race in four days of hard sailing, but my seasickness did not go away. A couple of weeks later I found out I was pregnant with my first child. I was so relieved I wasn't seasick!

Over the years I continued to race, but the favorite has always been the New Year's Day Cruising Regatta at Staniel Cay. Several races stand out in memory.

During the first or second regatta, we raced aboard Steve and Rita's sailboat, the *Rita J.*, carrying enough beer to match the weight of the crew. The race started with light winds, but as we rounded each buoy, it seemed to increase. The sails filled and the boat pushed forward and we were having a great sail. At one point, I went below decks to use the head, no easy business with the boat on its side. I heard a tremendous crash and was afraid to go topside, not knowing what had happened. When I finally climbed into the cockpit, I saw the mizzen mast and sail had been lashed to the deck, with the crew carrying on as if nothing happened. The stays had given way and the rig had collapsed. No one gave it much thought as the wind increased and the rail sliced through the choppy sea. We continued drinking and sailing with the mainsail and jib as if we never even had a mizzen. I can't remember who won the race or how we placed, but the beer was gone by the finish line.

In the early 1970s, I convinced Bob Chamberlain to buy a new mainsail and jib for the yacht club's 14-foot sailing dinghy acquired from a cruising yacht that no longer wanted it. I had sailed it a few times, and even though the boat seemed sluggish, I figured new sails would get her up to speed. Joan Mann's son, John Lawrence, who would later become commodore of the Nassau Yacht Club, offered to crew, and even fashioned a tiller extension out of a broom handle for the event.

The weather was not good. Even though we had a respectable start, the bigger yachts started gobbling us up, and then, in the midst of water spouts forming, we realized we had almost no speed at all and we were, in fact, sinking. It turns out the boat had a mysterious leak that allowed water to

Sailing into bad weather in the 14-foot dinghy.

fill the hull. We had to declare an emergency and be towed in. The race was later called due to the dangerous water spouts.

One year in the early 1980s, our whole family and lots of friends raced aboard *Tao*, a 56-foot trimaran that drew six feet. The wind was extremely light, and at one point, the current forced the heavy vessel to go backward. We had all the kids jump overboard and kick. We eventually abandoned the race and went to a beach.

By far the most significant race I sailed was in 1991.

In the months prior to the race, most of the young men on Staniel Cay helped rebuild the *Lady Muriel*, a Class A racing sloop that was originally from Long Island, Bahamas and raced by Hansel Miller of Staniel Cay in his younger days.

Unlike traditional sailing vessels, these sloops carry an incredibly tall mast and long boom in proportion to the length of the vessel, which is 28 feet with a 10-foot beam. The boom can be between 28 and 30 feet, and the mast can be as tall as 60 feet, which is stepped far forward. There is a relatively small jib in proportion to the mainsail, which is loose footed on the boom with a small headboard at the top. The sails are traditionally made of canvas. The ballast may be stones, lead, concrete, anything with weight, and is removable, so that it can be changed depending on weather or crew, which can be as many as twenty people in rough weather, or removed completely to haul the boat for repairs. The sloop has a long board, or pry, which can slide from one side to the other under a steel bracket in the deck. The crew hikes out on the pry to keep the boat level and to prevent it from tipping over when sailing to weather, much like leeboards on an inland lake racing scow.

Under the direction of Kenneth Rolle and Brooks Miller, *Lady Muriel* was rebuilt from the keel on up. Every weekend the boys were busy sanding, painting, sawing and fitting planks with absolutely no plan, just an innate sense of how a boat should be, look and feel. Her mast came from the tall pines of Abaco in the Northern Bahamas, known for its native boat building. When it was time to step the mast on *Lady M*, she was towed to Sampson Cay, where Marcus Mitchell onboard the freight vessel *M/V Victoria*, lifted the mast with the crane to set it into *Lady*

Lady Muriel *during the New Year's Regatta*

Muriel's deck, where it was secured in the bilge. Back at Staniel Cay, bars of lead ballast were lowered below decks until she sat majestically balanced in the water at Happy People dock.

As usual that year, I had waited until the last minute to find a boat to crew for the race. I was admiring *Lady Muriel*, and mentioned to Brooks Miller, the captain, that I still didn't have a boat to race on the next day. He said, "Sail with us. Be here at nine tomorrow morning." I asked if he was kidding, and was thrilled when he said he was serious. I hardly slept that night in anticipation of the race.

The Annual New Year's Day Cruising Regatta at Staniel Cay is different from conventional sailboat races. It's basically a fun outing, with area cruising boats challenging the local native entry. Only working sails, no spinnakers, are allowed. Because every boat is different, it's difficult or impossible to rate or handicap them, so usually the biggest, fastest boat wins.

The next morning I was at Happy People ready to sail, the only woman with at least a dozen guys in the crew. I listened to the friendly banter as we tacked before the race started. These were true sailors, highly skilled competitors, but there was something intangible that made a difference from any crew I had ever raced with in the past. The only description that comes to mind is "sing-songy."

There was a rhythm on the boat I had never experienced, almost like a ballet, with everyone smiling, in good spirits and not worrying if someone inched ahead. They instinctively knew what to do to regain their place. The spirit of the crew was joyful, not fierce, yet highly competitive. To this day, I have never experienced such camaraderie in a race. When tacking, those on the pry hanging out over the water had to scramble back on the boat, push the board to the other side and scramble back out in a matter of seconds to numerous shouts of encouragement to MOVE!

One of our challengers was *Windaway*. Over the years, the owners and their entourage would arrive from the States with the *Windaway* du jour ready to win, and each year, the challenge was to make sure she DIDN'T win, all in good spirits and fun. On this particular day, the race was delayed as the crew removed the engine propeller on *Windaway* to decrease drag on the hull to hopefully increase her speed and chance to win. Denis Posey's *Firebrand* crossed the finish line first that year, and *Lady Muriel* was second. I don't know how *Windaway* placed, but once again, she didn't win.

That night at the award's ceremony, Kenneth Rolle invited me to pick up the *Lady Muriel* second place trophy, and introduced me as the first woman to race on the new *Lady Muriel*.

The Prime Minister, Lynden O. Pindling, and several other government officials were present, as Staniel Cay was their favorite place for the New Year's celebration.

Another memorable Cruising Regatta was in 1996. Again, I didn't sign on a boat as crew until the last minute. I can't remember the name of the vessel, but as I stepped aboard, the owner turned her over to me, saying that I should take the helm as I had local knowledge. It was 50-some feet long and we only had four people for crew. We placed about midway in the fleet at the finish line and enjoyed the sail. As I maneuvered the vessel while the owner put down the anchor, we talked about our favorite sailboats. I mentioned how much I loved my Allied Seabreeze yawl of years ago.

He said, "That is one fine boat to sail. I and four other guys chartered one out of Nassau in 1970." He almost fell overboard when I said, "The *Toko Maru*." He had chartered our boat 26 years before I captained his boat in the race.

Now that I have my little 25-foot Cape Dory at the island, we have begun a new family tradition. I'm teaching the

Grandsom Gage and Capt. Chuck hoist Searene's *mainsail.*

grandkids to sail, and we now race *Searene* in the annual New Year's Day race. The first year we came in last, but we were also the smallest, and were dragging the outboard engine as we couldn't raise it up. It's not important to win. What IS important is to pass on the magic of sailing to my grandkids. I look forward to the day when Grammy can crew for THEM!

Original Serenity Cottage

By 1981, it became apparent that we needed our own place on the island, not only for the family, but for our pilots, who often had to overnight. We had been given the use of the big cottage at the yacht club any time the family visited, but as tourism increased, I found myself booking us out of a place to stay, reasoning that paying guests should have priority over us.

I don't know where the idea came from, because there was no premeditation on this thought, but one night I blurted out, "Why don't we buy Doc Saunder's place?" not even knowing if he would sell.

The next day, we called him in Connecticut. We had met him on several occasions, and we had flown him to the island along with Gil, his friend. Gil and Doc were old running mates of Bob Chamberlain, going back to the beginning of the yacht club. Doc's cottage, our original Serenity, was built at the same time as the first yacht club cottages, only it was much more primitive, basically a plywood shack. There were a few windows, but the porch only had wooden shutters, which opened Bahama-style, with a hinge on top and a stick propping them out from the bottom. The no-see-ums and

The original cottage porch and shutters.

mosquitoes had total access, along with roaches, spiders, hermit crabs...

Doc, who suffered from diabetes and some other problems, was going blind, so he used his "sundowner" hideaway less and less. In the previous seven years, he had allowed a local mechanic to live in the cottage for the price of just keeping it up. Had he been able to see, he would have been appalled at how it looked. A small sixteen-by-eight foot bunkhouse had been added, but other than that, only mini-

The cottage with new sliding doors, siding and original dock.

mum maintenance was done.

The cottage was connected to the yacht club generator system, so there was electricity, but in the course of a fall-out between the mechanic and the club, the power was cut off. He lived with kerosene lights, a gas stove and refrigerator.

When I finally got to take a look at the place, there were holes in the plywood floor, the kerosene had left a sooty film over everything, and it was NOT pretty.

But the price was. I won't say how much we paid, but Doc knew we were not in the chips and that it would help his old friends Bob and Joe if we had our own place. He had also heard of its condition. He checked with everyone on the island, including Rev. Kelly, to see if people wanted us there, and when we got overwhelming approval, he said he'd carry a mortgage at no interest, and that we could pay him each month as we were able, knowing that certain times of the year tourism was down as well as our income.

He wanted someone to love his little spot as he had loved it. We also told him he could visit any time he wanted to, and we even strung a rope on sturdy metal poles from the cottage to the dock so that he could feel his way down the uneven, rocky steps. He came a few times, but blindness and the amputation of his legs below the knees eventually put him in a nursing home. Sections of that same rope have been painted yellow and now trim my outdoor shower.

In the course of purchasing the cottage, the mechanic was given a letter from a real estate agent in Nassau, indicating that the property had been sold and that he was to vacate. We felt it better to use an agent, who was a friend, rather than have to deal with him personally. We knew it was not going to be a pleasant experience.

We soon found out just how upset he was. When we took possession of this plywood box, it was evident the place had not been cleaned in a very long time. I took one look at the kitchen and said, "Gut it." It was filthy and I would never have gotten it clean enough to my liking.

The outside was plywood with peeling yellow paint. We thought cedar shingles would make the place look nice, but because the cottage was so small, conventional shingles would have been out of proportion. To make the cottage more airtight, we put tarpaper on all the outside walls, then used cedar shim stock as shingles, the cheap bundles of wood carpenters use for wedging. Mindful of termites, we found an exterior stain that bugs hate, which was dutifully applied about every eight months for as long as the cottage stood.

Once we scraped off the gold-colored burlap that had been glued onto the inside walls, we discovered a collection of plywood, masonite, and other siding that was probably scrounged from the dump. It would have been impossible to paint, so we applied a neutral, textured wallpaper to hide the mess beneath.

The former occupant had broken every cabinet door and had racked the closet and outside doors. Short of knocking the place down, it had been destroyed.

We went to hook up the electric and discovered the transformer was gone. We also discovered that the cistern, the only supply of fresh water, had been drained. So, with no electric and no plumbing, we were back at the yacht club cottage until Trey could literally rebuild the place.

After ordering a new transformer and rigging a pump and pressure tank for water, Trey thought we would have electricity and running water. Wrong. All the wires had been cut and shoved far into the conduit or were gone altogether. When he turned on the water pump, there was a sprinkler system inside. There were holes in all the pipes! The cottage had to be totally re-wired and re-plumbed to be livable.

Trying to get legal satisfaction, more for Doc than ourselves, it turned out we had the same Nassau attorney as the mechanic and got absolutely nowhere. I think it broke Doc's heart to have this happen after helping someone for so many years, and he thought he was giving us more than what we

The original cottage and bunkhouse.

The cottage and bunkhouse after renovations.

got. We decided to move on and fix the place.

I thought a lot of Doc, a kind man with a gruff sense of humor.

At least twice a year, he would have his nurse call me, and he would want to know everything that was happening on the island. I would give him a report of individuals, how business was going, everything we had done to the cottage. We talked about kids and about personal problems and situations. We had a great friendship, but we were more like family. Years later, when his daughter notified me of his death, she said I would never know how much our relationship had meant to him, that it often kept him going. He, as I, had always looked forward to our calls.

Harold

Harold was also a special man, and our next door neighbor. Without him and his support of our air charter operation in the early days, we may not have had such a long relationship with the island.

He was a self-made, successful businessman from New Jersey, who loved the island as much as I have come to love it, mixed with occasional exasperation over getting things done. He told me the island would teach me patience beyond comprehension.

Harold and wife Isabel would stay for several months each year, and prior to his arrival in Fort Lauderdale, he would ship everything he wanted for his stay: food, hardware, motors, tools, PVC pipe fittings...his island storeroom became the island equivalent of Home Depot. It would take several flights to get everything to the island, and in the meantime, he would put in orders for yet more "stuff."

He was a generous man, not only with what he owned, but as a person. He was helpful, kind, sometimes a bit eccentric, but consistently loved life. He helped my husband put in our original dock, drilling holes in the coral with his special drill for eight-by-eight foot pilings, and was an endless source of information.

Many mornings he would knock at our door and present us with fresh baked cinnamon rolls or coffee cake.

A world traveler, he would share salmon he caught in the Arctic, caribou from Alaska, moose or buffalo from Montana. One of his specialties was smoked barracuda. He would catch the smaller ones that were still edible, put them in the smoker, and wait for them to be just right. Then he'd share with anyone wanting to taste something a little different, yet delectable.

He could fix anything, and understood how everything worked, so he was a constant source of information when a problem arose and the right parts weren't available.

Harold loved big-boy toys. He had two early versions of the six-wheel ATV with big balloon tires on fiberglass frames

Harold's six-wheeler on the ocean beach.

that could handle our roadless, rough terrain as well as the water. We would often load up the six-wheelers and head to the ridge for a picnic, which generally took most of the day. He'd drive the kids up and down the beach, into the water, up the dunes and back in the big buggies. Those were fun times.

In the early 1980s, when satellite television was in its infancy, someone in that business visited the island from Illinois. Mike convinced us that we could get satellite television (we didn't even have electricity on the island, only individual generators). Others argued we were out of the "footprint" and that it couldn't possibly work. The deal was that Mike would ship all the components needed to put in the system, send a couple of technicians to put it together, and if it worked, we would give him free vacations at Serenity for a couple of years.

It wasn't long before sections of a 12-foot dish arrived, along with numerous boxes and wire. Not thinking it would work, we brought over the cheapest 19-inch television we could find. When all the components were on the island, Mike arrived with his crew. We didn't have a good location for the dish on our little plot of land, so Harold told us to put it on his

Daughter Coral and the first sat dish on the island.

land just off our driveway. The crew feverishly put everything together with stainless steel bolts and by the end of the first day, WE HAD TELEVISION!

Word quickly spread, and everyone in the village came to see this new phenomenon. They lined up chairs outside just like in a movie theater, we made popcorn, and everyone watched the show. The technicians had to search for the working satellites, but everyone was happy. Whenever we were on the island, village children spent Saturday mornings watching cartoons at Serenity. It was the only day they were broadcast in the early days before 24/7 channels for kids.

At that time you didn't subscribe to channels. You either got satellite TV or you didn't. We would be watching a channel, thinking it was the evening news, when suddenly it would be rewound and we'd be watching them edit what we had just seen.

When the U.S. raced the World Cup in Australia in 1983, we tuned in to the local Australian broadcast rather than the U.S. ESPN feed, and listened to the crew chat during commercials, the cameras still on the boats while someone asked for a beer. The Cup was won by the challenger, *Australia II*, ending the longest United States winning streak in the history of the sport. We had been able to watch every tack of every race because of our wonderful new dish.

In appreciation to Harold for giving us the land for the dish and helping to put the base into the rock, we hooked him into our new sat system so he could also enjoy television. The only problem was that he had to watch what we watched. You couldn't have multiple receivers with one dish back then.

On occasion, Harold would call us on the VHF radio, requesting we switch the channel to "you know." Since everyone on the island had a VHF and knew what that meant, they knew he wanted to watch the Playboy channel. A little while later, Harold would call back and say, "Okay," and we would switch back to whatever we were watching. Isabel would just laugh when anyone asked her about it.

In the mid-1980s, Geraldo, as I recall in-between wives and jobs, sailed into Staniel Cay. The Super Bowl was the next day and he wanted to watch the game. He was told there was only one TV on the island, so he and his friends were our unexpected, but interesting, guests at Serenity that afternoon.

Freight Boats

Vivian Rolle gave me a bit of history on the mail boats for Staniel Cay. In the early days, prior to 1967, mail, freight and groceries for Staniel Cay and Black Point originally went to Farmer's Cay, the first headquarters for the central Exuma Cays, even though as now, the mail boat could not get close enough to the island to dock. Small boats have always taken freight to shore.

"We had to go all the way to Farmer's Cay to collect mail, supplies, or government business," she said. Later, the headquarters moved to Black Point.

Staniel Cay Express *passing Thunderball rocks.*

"If weather wasn't good, everything had to stay in a warehouse at Farmer's Cay. Often, by the time we got there, the rats had eaten most of our rice and flour. We didn't have outboard boats at that time. We had to sail up there to pick up everything, or someone coming down would be kind enough to bring our mail or groceries, but then we still had to go and pay the freight."

While Americans normally refer to north as "up " and south as "down," the Bahamians base those two directions on the prevailing wind. Since it is from the southeast, one goes "down" to Nassau and "up" to Georgetown.

Because of the inconvenience of getting supplies to Staniel Cay, Captain Rolly Gray decided "to better the cays" with a shallow draft vessel that could come dockside. The *Staniel Cay Express* was launched in 1967, giving Staniel Cay its first direct, reliable mail, freight and passenger service.

There were several "mails" after the *Staniel Cay Express*: *Lady Blanche*, *The Grand Master* (still in service to Georgetown), the *Etienne and Cephas* (mentioned in the Millennium chapter), *Lady Francis*, and more recently, *MV Captain C*, which has advanced to freezer, cold storage and air conditioned cabins, with a fairly reliable weekly schedule to the

M/V Captain C. *passing Thunderball rocks.*

island and points beyond Staniel Cay. She is under way almost the entire week from Nassau south to the Ragged Islands and back, with a couple of days for loading in Nassau.

***

Aboard the Captain C

In April 2008, I booked passage on the *Captain C* to the Ragged Islands, located in the Jumento Cays, about 60 miles north of Cuba and about 85 miles west of Great Exuma. Capt. Etienne Maycock, originally from Duncan Town in the Ragged Islands, was the captain. I wanted to compare the voyage with my previous ventures, and I am happy to report it was a wonderful, educational trip, and one I would recommend to anyone looking for adventure.

If regatta is religion, the mail boats provide the rhythm of

Freight on the dock at Staniel Cay.

the Bahamas. Life revolves around and depends on the freight boat schedual.

As we departed Staniel Cay, which has a very shallow channel to the government dock, Capt. Etienne almost put the bow on shore as he maneuvered the 120-foot dark blue steel hull drawing 7.5 feet in an area that rapidly went to less than three feet outside the narrow channel. If he arrives at low tide, he anchors out until about half-tide, and upon leaving, he often has to wait for the tide to rise.

Looking back toward the dock, there were pallets of soft drinks, several brands of beer, liquor, lumber, propane tanks, paper goods, with small boats coming to pick up goods for Compass Cay, Sampson Cay, Fowl Cay, and Overyonder Cay. Locals backed pickup trucks and golf carts onto the dock to load up with personal affects and groceries and goods for the small stores. Everyone was coming and going, clearing the dock in a haphazard, yet ritualistic beat, to smiles and small talk, lending a hand where needed, catching up on local gossip.

We took the shallow bank side to Black Point, five miles to the south, and a boat and pickup truck were the first items hoisted ashore as I scanned the dock for familiar faces. Then came pallets of groceries, bottled water, propane tanks, 55-gallon fuel drums (although there are about 600 residents on Black Point, the north end of Great Guana Cay, there is no gasoline or diesel fuel available), household furnishings including two couches and several large chairs, all picked up by crane and deposited on the government dock, then whisked away in pickup trucks.

Willie, husband of my wonderful housekeeper Betty, came aboard to say hello, and I waved and chatted with Mary,

Unloading cargo at Black Point.

an American woman who has lived on Black Point for many years and whom I've known since the 1970s. She used to fly with us to Staniel Cay, usually showing up with several miscellaneous "carpet" bags, sending my husband to the edge of anxiety. Every flight, he'd explain that she had not chartered the plane, that she'd only bought a seat, and he would ask her to choose what was absolutely necessary for that particular flight. One time she paid us with gallons of honey from her Florida bee hives. We always made sure her belongings "reached."

In a couple of hours, we were again on our way, out Dotham Cut into Exuma Sound heading for Little Farmer's Cay, where we anchored close to the island. Several small boats came alongside, and pallets of concrete, household goods, fuel and construction materials were hoisted down, changing the water line considerably on a couple of small vessels burdened with cement.

Then it was out Farmer's Cay Cut to Goat Cay, owned by two famous American country singers. We were able to dock after anchoring a couple of small boats we had in tow, and slowly approached the dock, where we offloaded 32 tons (16 full pallets) of concrete, plus lumber. When we were ready to leave, the tide had fallen considerably, and we churned up sand departing the dock. Two of the Farmer's Cay boats wanting a tow to the Jumentos to gather conch met us as we picked up the little boats we had anchored. One tied to the back of the *Captain C* and the other one came alongside to take the freight for Barraterre on Great Exuma, a regular stop for the

M/V Captain C *underway, heading south.*

Captain C. He headed south to deliver and pick up the return cargo, and we met up with the boat after dark on the banks as we headed toward the Jumento Cays.

At some point during the night, we dropped the Farmer's Cay fishermen near Flamingo Cay and we went on to Ragged Island.

I couldn't even see Duncan Town from the *Captain C* as

Duncan Town harbor.

we anchored off nearby Hog Cay Point as it was too shallow to get any closer to Ragged Island. Once in a little boat, we headed for the two-mile long dredged channel fringed by mangroves on the right and a mound of sand with various vegetation on the left. The sides sloped down and we threaded the center, staying in the narrow channel that was too shallow for any freight boat. I was amazed at the green color, and later learned it was algae, caused by lack of tidal flow through the harbor, where fishermen have cleaned conch and fish for years. At one time the harbor was so clear children could swim in it, but no longer. The natives told me about a government dredging project that will eventually provide a deeper channel for freight boats, but nothing has happened as yet.

I was told that occasionally shallow draft landing barges come from Nassau through the channel to the dock with big items such as vehicles and fuel drums.

As I stepped out of the little boat at Duncan Town, I heard roosters crow in the distance, but the island was basically very quiet. I took a few photos of the harbor, then climbed a rather steep road up to the village. Maxine Wallace, whom I had met on the *Captain C* returning from Nassau with her husband, Rev. Daniel Wallace, her nephew and two little Shih Tzu dogs, had told me I could walk everywhere, but it was extremely hot and I knew I didn't have the stamina, so I asked Latoya, who had also ridden the *Captain C* from Nassau back home with us, if she would show me the island in her golf cart.

I was amazed at the old abandoned houses. Between Maxine, the Rev and Latoya, I learned that at one time five hundred people lived in Duncan Town. Because of its distance from Nassau, trade in the old days was with Cuba, the Dominican Republic and Haiti. After Castro in Cuba and Papa Doc in Haiti, all trade stopped and Duncan Town began to die, with the young people forced to find work elsewhere to survive. Now there were only fifty people.

Salt was one of the main industries when the island thrived, and the salt ponds and flats are still there, although only a few of the elders now harvest the salt. We did take about five hundred pounds on the *Captain C* to go to Nassau, but that was only a grain compared to what was shipped years ago.

Abandoned homes at Duncan Town, termite nest on right.

When we arrived at a beautiful, deserted, white sand horseshoe shaped beach, Latoya said there were still many "finds" if I wanted to beachcomb, but there wasn't enough time. She also pointed out a gate that could manage the water on the salt flats, no longer in operation. If it rained, the gate would be opened to allow the fresh water to go into the sea. As the flats evaporated and salt was gathered, the gate would then allow salt water to enter to continue the "crop." It is hard, back-breaking work.

Duncan Town salt flats.

We drove along abandoned roads, tufts of green poking through cracks and potholes, fringed by small, abandoned homes, some with large termite nests claiming what was left of a roof, while others were consumed by the surrounding bush.

At the end of one of the roads was the village cemetery, built in 1926. An earlier cemetery is so overgrown it is no longer visible from the road. I was amazed at the size of the new one, completely walled, filled with white sand and sprouting lily-like plants. The headstones were chiseled, and it was obvious that this sacred ground was well tended, with

Duncan Town cemetary.

what is known as "Lover's Leap" islands just offshore. It was a peaceful, reverent setting for family members now passed.

In contrast to the old, Duncan Town has a relatively new police station, and a well tended telephone building boasting a huge modern communications dish. There are a couple of newer buildings with a total of eight guest rooms, but at this time, nothing was open.

As lunchtime approached, I asked if there was a restaurant and Latoya informed me that nothing was open at the time, although her mother, Sheila, ran the Fisherman's Lounge. She smiled and drove me to a rather new home, where upon entering, I was thrilled to see Erica Gray of Staniel Cay, now married to the man in charge of Bahamas Electric on Ragged Island. A huge flat screen television was showing a DVD of Captain Rolly Gray's recent funeral, which had just arrived on the *Captain C*. We talked about her grandfather being the Bahama's celebrated Grand Master, of good times past and present, as I ate chicken, peas and rice and salad.

Next we visited the school, built for the many children who once attended. Now there were only nine students and one teacher. A wall of the play area showed the major islands of the country.

One of my observations was how different cisterns were built compared to those on Staniel Cay. In Duncan Town, they all had pitched, shingled roofs. On Staniel Cay and other islands in the Exumas, the tops are flat concrete. While rain water is still caught off roofs and stored, the island does have a government reverse osmosis system. Another difference was in the many types of boats I saw, including a very colorful Jamaican canoe, long and narrow.

Jamaican fishing canoe.

I also noticed fish nets strung between trees and on front porches, makeshift hammocks for enjoying a lazy afternoon. Besides the many chickens and roosters strutting about, there were also sounds and smells of pigs and goats, which came to their fences out of curiosity to welcome this stranger.

There are three little churches in Duncan Town: the Church of God and Prophecy, an Anglican church and a Baptist church. With the Church of God minister in Nassau earning a living and the Baptist church pastor elderly and blind, Rev. Daniel Wallace gives the sermon for all three churches on Sunday, everyone gathering at one of the them.

Although Ragged Island has a runway with a bar boasting an old DC-3 hull that looks like it landed on the roof, at this time there are no regular flights to the island. Hopefully this will change, with possibly two flights from Nassau each week. There is also talk of development on adjacent Little Ragged Island, with the projection of a golf course near the airstrip on the larger island. It was difficult to envision this level of progress on a place so lost in time, but it would be wonderful to see the community revived.

The Rev and Maxine filled my head with island history.

The first settlers came from England more than 100 years ago, and today's generation reflects the names: Monroes, Moxey, Wilson, Lockhart, and later Maycock and Wallace.

Maxine was one of fourteen children, eleven girls and three boys. Her grandmother died on the island at age 88 and her mother at 85. Her grandmother had the only drug store on the island, and now Maxine carries on the tradition with Wallace's Drugs and Grocery.

Salt became a major industry on Ragged Island, along with plat, conch, lobster and fish, which were exported to Cuba and Haiti as well as to Nassau.

The Rev said the Chinese in Nassau would buy much of the conch to make medicine, boiling it down to a jelly, then adding chemicals to make a rubbing compound to be shipped to China.

Dried conch is still exported to New York and Canada as well as China through merchants in Nassau.

Maxine and her husband love to go conching. After extracting the animals from their shells, they beat, or "bruise" them to tenderize the meat before salting and hanging them on a line to dry overnight. By morning they are ready to cook or to ship in drums. During the winter they let them cure a bit longer and have to make sure no rain water falls on them during the curing process.

Because the Ragged Islands are so pristine, many yachts come each year to enjoy the tranquility, and fishermen come from all over the Bahamas to fish, gather conch and crawfish. Unfortunately, there are poachers from other countries who take conch and crawfish, even during the closed season. Because the Raggeds are so far from the rest of the Bahamas, it's difficult to patrol.

There is also the remnants of drug trafficking. An abandoned, relatively new and expensive Contender with twin outboards was part of the cargo loaded on the *Captain C* to be delivered to the police and customs in Nassau for investigation.

Because there is so little industry left on the Ragged Islands, there are no trades people in Duncan Town: no plumber, carpenter, mason, mechanic, tile installer or electrician. Residents wait for months for service and construction people to come from Nassau or other islands, so everything looks like a work in progress.

But those who stay enjoy the peace and quiet while hoping for the promised dredging of the canal and development of the island. Duncan Town is a happy, easy going, friendly little place waiting to share its many riches with visitors. I feel blessed to have had the opportunity to meet them and to learn so much history in one day. I definitely look forward to a return visit and would recommend the trip to anyone seeking adventure.

As we headed out the channel from Duncan Town to board the *Captain C* for the return trip, we were treated to an awesome sunset, a perfect end to a delightful day. Passing a small island I noticed a cross, and was told a Catholic priest had been shipwrecked and drowned there. In the distance, the *Captain C* had its lights on welcoming everyone back.

We waited a few more hours for Capt. Etienne to check on his family and goat farm in Duncan Town, then began the trip back to Staniel Cay. About 2 a.m. the boat slowed down and I realized we were at Flamingo Cay picking up the two Farmer's Cay fishing boats, this time loaded with about 1,200 conch. We once again had a dog aboard, Sheba, a beautiful black lab, who was riding the boat to Nassau. Her owner departed by small boat at Barraterre to fly to Nassau and would meet her there. We also had a crate of chickens and a

Memorial cross off Duncan Town.

rooster on the back deck.

Instead of offloading cargo, we picked up items bound for Nassau from Farmer's Cay and then Black Point: plat for the straw market, empty propane tanks, empty fuel tanks, etc. We also accumulated a couple more boats both on deck and to tow behind.

While the trip was a lot of fun, it felt good to see Staniel Cay from Exuma Sound and to enter Big Rock Cut, knowing I was home.

Would I do it again? Absolutely! Riding the mail boat gave me a new connection to the Bahamas. I expanded my horizons, made new friends and felt the watery pulse of this beautiful island country.

***

I had several "firsts" aboard the *Captain C* besides the journey itself. I ate grits for the first time, served with sausages for breakfast prepared by cook Ronnie, and I learned to play dominoes, slapping the tiles down like a pro after my initiation. While meals were provided, they were sparse during loading and offloading, with many passengers and crew preparing their own meals in the large galley. Chicken and pork chops, as well as stewed fish, eggs, tuna and egg salad were served under way. I was glad I had tucked in some fruit, a small jar of peanut butter, some crackers and a box of cereal, as I did miss a couple of meals.

Since there were so few passengers, I was given my own stateroom with a window on the top deck. There were three bunks on either side. The first night I had a wonderful breeze, but on the return, I requested the air conditioning be turned on as the breeze was now on the other side of the boat and I couldn't sleep. The main deck had separate men's and women's bathrooms with a shower. The upper deck had only one bathroom, but it had a lock for privacy.

Rat Tales

While an island may be a romantic vacation getaway, it is never without a healthy rodent population. This is not something you advertise in brochures to lure guests. The situation is not what it was in the early years, but in the past, heavy rains would often send the unwanted critters to seek refuge in the club, cottages and private homes. It was a constant battle of man against beast, but it was always better to trap them rather than poison them. If they died in the walls, the stench would last for months. But the problem with trapping meant that an unsuspecting tourist might stumble on the evidence. Welcome to Paradise.

***

One off-season when few people were on the island, our charter boat friends Skeeze and Maggie were with us on the island, as well as the Chamberlains and Hochers. We were all enjoying a short vacation from tourists, boating and having beach picnics with the kids.

Sadie was behind the original U-shaped bar of the Staniel

Cay Yacht Club, where, a few years earlier, people sat on the dozen stools drinking on the honor system. The pool table was in one corner of the club, and chairs made from old wine barrels so heavy you couldn't move them, were around tables made from discarded wire reels. The roof of the club was corrugated steel, which leaked in spots where Captain Bob, a little on the tipsy side at the time, once fired at rats.

To hide the rusting roof, palm thatch was nailed to all the beams and cross-beams, giving the bar and restaurant the look of a thatched hut. Every year the hotel inspector would come from Nassau and take a look at the drying thatch. Bob and Joe would produce a document indicating it had been sprayed with fireproof material, and they would be signed off for another year, winking at each other as the inspector left. Thank God there was never a fire.

Because we were on vacation, the rum flowed freely, and we had the time to catch up on family stories. I was listening to Donna Chamberlain, who could talk nonstop, sipping my

Original SCYC bar and barrel chairs.

rum and trying to pay attention. I had on a new lime green pantsuit. It was early evening. Sadie left the bar for the ladies room, and Donna talked on. I heard something above my head in the thatch, and asked Donna what it was. She never heard me, just kept on talking, when I looked up to see what the commotion was all about. Two huge rats, frigging in the rigging, so to speak, fell right on my head! I screamed so loudly Sadie was afraid to come out of the ladies room and all the men came running in from the dock to see what had happened. Donna never stopped talking. In the meantime, I tumbled over three of the barrel chairs, tore holes in my brand new outfit and started crying. Donna was talking as if I were still sitting next to her on the barstool. Sadie said she almost turned white when I screamed. I was a mess, so I did what was normal back in my drinking days. I drank enough rum to get me back to "normal." The big cottage at the club, where we were staying, had a reputation for harboring rats, so in order to sleep, I always made sure I was on the verge of pass-

Original cottages and trees which were cleared for the swimming pool.

ing out before hitting the bed.

After dinner, Trey and Skeeze went back to the big cottage to check on the kids, already in bed. As they left, the door slammed, my back to it. What I didn't see was that Skeeze opened the door again. A second later something again hit my head from above. I went into hysterics. Skeeze had tossed a pack of cigarettes into the thatch so it would fall on me. He thought it was extremely funny. I did not. I spent the rest of our vacation plotting how to get even with him (Sadie offered to help me find hermit crabs to put in his bed), possibly maiming him for life, and I never again sat at the bar without an eye to the overhead thatch.

***

There was a time when the rats really got out of hand at the club. It was a year when we had a lot of rain, and although the rats are known to live in wet places such as sewers, they also like to sample the good life. The club seemed like a popular place, so a family of rats with all their relatives decided to move in.

After my incident with the rats falling on my head, people were a bit wary until they had enough to drink where it didn't matter WHAT was overhead. The thatch covered up a lot of the unknown, but occasionally, patrons would watch rats scurrying along the rafters between the kitchen and the bar, as if they didn't know if they wanted to eat or drink, but definitely having a free run of the place without running a tab.

Sometimes Capt. Bob would have enough of them. He'd pull out his .22 from under the bar, take as careful aim as possible in his rum-induced state, and fire off a few bullets to scare the rats away. Occasionally he'd get one, but not very often. What he DID get was the metal roof, evident the next time it rained. Then one of the workers would be sent up a ladder with a caulking gun to try to plug the holes. Eventually he was convinced to keep the gun somewhere else. No one wanted to be his next target.

***

During one of our "rat" seasons, when they were unusually brave and bold, I was lying in bed, a pull-out sofa in the living area of the original Serenity cottage watching TV. For some reason I don't recall, I was on the island and the rest of the family was back in the States.

I heard a persistent scratching sound where the TV cables came inside from the satellite dish on the roof, next to the kitchen cabinets. When some of the insulation we had stuffed into the hole began to fall on the counter below, it got my attention, and soon I saw a couple of beady eyes in a rat face emerge.

I stood on the bed, pointed at the rat and yelled at the top of my voice, "You son of a bitch, get out of my house." The rat looked me as if to say, "Well okay, if that's the way you feel," turned around and crawled back out. Score one for me.

The next day I got the good expanding stuff you spray from a can and over-plugged the hole on both sides. That took care of THAT rat entry. Who needs to adjust cables anyway?

But of course, the rat stories continued. They are clever, hungry, disgusting creatures who believe they are superior to the human race. I'm sure they've been here a lot longer than we have.

My next rat story takes place when the whole family was enjoying a vacation. The kids were in the bunkhouse next to the cottage, and we were settled in for the night. About midnight, I heard the telltale scratching of something (I knew what that something was!) trying to get in where the telephone and VHF radio antennas entered the house on the south side of the living room over the closet (the previous TV entry was on the north side by the kitchen). I heard it come in, walk along the wood beam, drop down on the kitchen counter and rummage for a snack. I was paralyzed with fear, woke up my husband to tell him about our intruder, and he told me to go back to sleep. I was bug-eyed for hours, until I heard the rat go back out the same way it came in.

The next night I loaded up a trap with peanut butter and left it on the counter where I thought he (why do we assume rats are "he's?") would again drop down from the beam.

Sure enough, right on schedule at midnight, I heard the scratching, the patter across the beam, and the drop to the counter. I think Mr. Rat seriously thought about eating the tempting peanut butter, but was more fickle that night and decided to search for something else. After what seemed like an hour, he hadn't yet found something to his liking, or perhaps had found a cracker that would taste better with peanut butter, so he cautiously approached the trap. As he put his foot down (I assume it was a foot), the trap went off, sending him flying up to the beam and out of the cottage. I flipped on the lights, woke up my husband, pointed to the trap and said, "There, are you satisfied we've got rats?" He told me it wouldn't come back again that night and to get some sleep.

Night three I was ready. I watched the clock for midnight.

The trap was carefully set and slightly concealed to try and outwit my home invader. On cue, Mr. Rat came in through his customary opening (I couldn't reach the hole to fill with foam and my husband wasn't taking this burglar seriously), walked across the beam, this time dislodging a wire that connected the stereo speakers from one side of the cottage to the other. He dropped down on the counter and thought, "Hmm...cheese AND peanut butter. What a feast!" He just couldn't resist, so delved in, at which point the trap caught his hand in the cookie jar, if you want to make that analogy.

But his head and the rest of him was intact. The trap, now connected to the rat, flopped around on the counter, finally woke up my husband who STILL didn't want to do anything, and fell to the floor, where the rat wriggled free and scurried under the stove. Great. Now I had a wounded rat hiding in my kitchen where I couldn't see him. My husband went back to sleep and I plotted, wide-eyed, what to do.

I decided that maybe rats weren't as smart as we think. I reset the trap, again with peanut butter and cheese, careful to not get too close to the stove, and used a mop handle to position it where I figured the rat could see it, and definitely smell it. I assumed he was still hungry and would need all the strength he could get to escape. I climbed back into bed and waited. And waited. And waited. About 3 a.m., Mr. Rat decided the coast was clear, felt brave since he'd escaped the trap twice, and became overconfident. The trap nailed him, but he still wasn't dead and again, the horrible flopping sound of the trap on tile again woke up my husband. I yelled at him, "Do something, for God's sake!"

That's when I found out his supposed unconcern about the rat was really FEAR. He reluctantly got up, I gave him the mop, which was one of those sponge things with a good metal edge for scraping goo off the floor and squeezing water out when you pulled the tingum on the stick, and he whopped that rat something fierce.

Not wanting to touch Mr. Rat, he got the dust pan, scooped him up trap and all, and tossed them both into the flower bed outside.

The next day there was no sign of the rat OR the trap. Something, maybe a hungry tomcat, had absconded in the night with our catch.

We had no midnight visitors for the rest of our vacation.

***

Years later, a young man who had lived with me in Fort Lauderdale while attending school to learn English, wanted to visit the island after hearing so much about it. He had a free weekend, the kids were no longer living at home, so we flew to the island for a short visit to my cottage.

As I was showing him the island, we eventually came to the yacht club, where there was quite a commotion going on by the dock. Some of the native guys were chiding each other about doing something, and there was tension mounting. The nurse, our beloved Mary Lou, was talking to the group, and all I heard was, "The man's dead. It's just a body." The responses were varied, but all added up to the same conclusion. No one was going to touch a dead body. "Not me, Mon." "Me neider." "Gits someone else."

I asked Mary Lou what had happened. She had been called to a boat at anchor early morning where a man had already died of a heart attack. She needed to have his body brought to the clinic so the commissioner flying in from Georgetown could declare him dead so the body could be flown to Nassau for autopsy, where the coroner could again declare him dead so the family could then claim his body.

(I have a standing order to all the local pilots. If I die on the island, prop me up in the co-pilot's seat and head for the U.S. Tell them I was alive when you left.)

The man's wife and another boater had helped Mary Lou get the body in a small boat to the yacht club, where it was wrapped in a blanket and filled a large portion of the dinghy. The man's wife was hysterical and in need of a sedative, pleading with Mary Lou to help her and what should she do?

The local Bahamian young men have a thing about dead bodies, as if death were catching, or they'd be forever branded if they touched a cold body, or their hair would go straight...whatever, they weren't about to touch a dead body.

Armin made the mistake of volunteering to help. The local guys looked at him as if he was touched by voodoo, but encouraged him.

"Yeah, Mon, you brave, Mon, go to it, Mon."

A couple of other visitors said they would help, and the body was heaved out of the small dinghy, awkwardly carried, and lifted onto a pickup truck, which had been backed to the dock to where the concrete ended and the dock planks began. The body was then driven to the clinic, where Mary Lou had cranked the air conditioning to low, because that was the best she could do as a temporary morgue.

Armin got high-fives all weekend as the brave foreign guy who wasn't afraid of dead people.

That was day one of only two nights on the island.

That night, Mr. Rat decided to grace my threshold via one

of the forever changing holes in my not-so-airtight cottage.

Armin was sleeping in the bunkhouse. In the middle of the night, I couldn't stand it any longer. The rat had been rummaging through the closet, had taken a tour of the kitchen, and was fraying my nerves. I got up, turned on all the lights, and set a couple of traps. I lucked out with a dumb rat that night, because it soon took the peanut butter bait in the trap in the closet. There has got to be a better rat trap design. I again ended up with a wounded rat flopping around in the closet.

I woke Armin out of a dead sleep, pleading with him to come and help me with a rat. He rolled his eyes and said something about Paradise, but followed me into the cottage. The rat had finally stopped thrashing and appeared to be dead. Armin poked it with a broom and indeed pronounced him dead. He picked up the trap (so brave...he didn't use the dust pan), and tossed the rat and trap into the flower bed, saying he'd retrieve the trap in the morning after dumping the rat overboard.

Once again, no rat and no trap the next morning. I wondered if something stalked the rats that visit Serenity, knowing there would be an easy meal tossed into the bush during the night.

The second day and night were uneventful and Armin took some good island stories back to Germany.

I bought a large supply of rat traps.

Termites

The rats may like to gnaw and eat everything from paper to plastic and food, but it's the termites who win as the most destructive form of life on the island. I had heard stories, but never quite understood how voracious these tenacious little dots of life can be.

When the original cottage was habitable, we invited some friends for the weekend. We cooked a great dinner Saturday night, then we all went to the yacht club to party into the late hours. We all came back a little less aware than we were before we left.

The next morning, battling the leftover rum in my system, I went to the kitchen to fix breakfast, thinking if I got enough protein in everyone the moans and groans would stop and we could enjoy beaching and snorkeling after church services.

I think they heard my scream all the way to the village. It certainly woke up the rest of our crew, who came running in from outside.

OVERNIGHT, termites had invaded my kitchen. Wherever it was dark, away from the light, there were mud tunnels over dishes, inside the creases of the drawers, over the Tupperware, in the silverware tray, along the cabinet doors, marching over plates and glasses and circling cleaning supplies. Close the cabinet doors and drawers and they were nonexistent. Open them and it was a horror movie.

Trey knew that the Rev had the good poison for the burrowing insects that ate wood and pooped out their tunnels as they moved along, so he ran to the village to see if he could borrow enough to kill the army invading us. Church was delayed that morning as everyone came to see this remarkable phenomenon. People had seen damage occur over days and weeks, but never this much overnight.

Our guests helped us clean everything out of the kitchen, watching the white termites scramble for darkness as we broke up their covered roads. Trey was right there with the poison, careful not to get any on food or items that would be used for food. I remember having goose bumps all over looking at these seemingly harmless insects and realizing their destructive nature.

It took all day to rid the cottage of the termites, but there was enough poison inside and outside to discourage them for a long time. Every time I returned to the cottage, I would look for possible termite invasion.

The worst time of the year is the rainy season. The termites need water, so if there is a good source, they eat more, reproduce more, and create these half-inch wide poop tunnels as they chomp along wood beams, plywood, even garden mulch. Many old structures in south Florida were originally built of Dade pine, which is an extremely hard wood (you can't nail without drilling first) that is impervious to termites. Our main support columns in the cottage were

Dade pine, so at least the roof was held up. Termites also don't like pressure treated wood, but if it's old and the chemicals have dissipated, they'll find a way through. Many times I've had to throw out plywood for hurricane shutters because of termites making their home between the sheets.

Several times when I arrived, the boat house was filled with the termite runs. It was a constant battle to keep them away. They even marched their tunnels over Christmas ornaments and lights stored in the rafters.

I soon realized that putting poison out was not the most efficient or expeditious way to eliminate them. Finding the nest is the best solution, so I have been known to crawl through the tangle of bushes on and around my property looking for the brown mounds that can be on the ground or attached to a tree or shrub. These are not small items. They can grow, if not destroyed, to three feet high and two feet in diameter.

Once as I was poisoning a nest and watching the tiny little buggers scramble, I thought I'd pour some into a dead tree. As the poison seeped down the hollow trunk, a horde of huge termites, another variety that looks more like big ants, poured out, rapidly climbing on anything to get away from certain death. They were so fast I found myself swatting them on my arms. They had marched right up the nozzle of the sprayer and on to me! I've mellowed over the years, so my screams and shrieks have turned to cussing and swearing while battling the buggers. It's a non-ending war, but I've personally taken it upon myself to destroy any termite nest I see anywhere on the island.

***

One of my favorite termite stories took place in 2003. My mother was visiting the island, and had accompanied me in the golf cart to the dump, which I have referred to as our local K-Mart. When we arrived that day, the merchandise went way beyond discount-store finds. Right there, in the middle of maggot infested garbage bags, discarded lumber, old batteries and bottles, stood an upright piano.

I knew it came from the yacht club. I knew there were talks of termites, but looking at that piano, it looked perfect. It was even relatively in tune. My mother started playing, and when others came, we were all laughing so hard we could barely catch our breath. My Mom convinced me that I should have this piano for my new Serenity, scheduled to be built the following year. I had nine years of piano lessons as a child and really enjoyed playing. I switched to the guitar when I was 18 because I couldn't lug a piano around. We looked over this magnificent instrument in the dump, searching for any termite damage. Everyone who came to discard trash while we were there also took part in this examination process, and it was declared by all that the piano was termite free.

I asked Barry, who owns a home on the island with the lower level designed for laundry, storage and garage, if I could store this lovely find at his house until I could move it into my new house when it was built. He looked at it, and said, "Sure." He even helped find someone with a truck. As the word spread that the dump piano had a new home, several of the local boys came to help load it in the truck. As we drove to South Staniel to Barry's house, one of the native guys plunked away and they sang and danced the reggae as the truck rolled along.

The piano was put in Barry's lower level, and a couple of

The piano still played...who would have suspected termites?

weeks later, he went back to the states.

About three months later, I received a frantic, emergency call from him. THE ENTIRE LOWER LEVEL OF HIS HOUSE HAD TERMITES! All his plywood hurricane shutters, spare wood, everything MADE of wood, was damaged. Mercifully, they had not yet reached the structural beams above supporting the house floor. The piano was again hauled to the dump and promptly burned. This time no one sang.

It was a very expensive piano.

Karl

In the early 1970s, Karl lived the life of a hermit on South Staniel's beautiful beach facing the sunset, in his small wood framed house. He had no generator, hence no electric, and fresh water came from his cistern, filled by rain caught off the roof.

Late fall each year, he would arrive in Fort Lauderdale from Connecticut. He would call from the airport, inform us that he was in town, and ask how fast could we pick him up. It's important to understand that (a) we were a charter air service, not a road taxi, (b) we were not a hotel and (c), our customers were told when and where to meet us for their flight to the island.

None of this meant anything to Karl. He expected us to pick him up at the airport, give him lodging and meals, and take him to the plane when it was time. This was all, he decided, included in the price of his seat to the island. Nevermind that he was wealthy. He just spent as little as possible to get by. He grew what he could on the island, tomatoes, herbs and other vegetables, and caught fish.

We humored him year after year, picking him up, putting

him up, flying him to and from the island. The challenge was to get him to the States in time for a flight back to Connecticut the same day. Otherwise, it meant putting him up for another night. We didn't mind because he was an interesting old fellow, who was originally from, of all places, Fond du Lac, Wisconsin, a few miles from where I grew up. This, of course, made us family. How could I ever say "no" to him?

Another expectation was that if his wife, Mary, sent a message or package, we would deliver it in person. In those days, prior to telephone service, this meant my husband had to physically find him on the island. Back then, as now, every home had a VHF radio for communicating with each other, as well as boats in the area. But not Karl. That was too fan-dan-gle for him. My husband would have to make time between flights to walk to his house and deliver the message or package. As business increased and time became precious, he finally told Karl that he would no longer be delivering messages in person, that he was to get a radio, and turn it on when he saw the plane land. If there was a message or package, he would be told and could come to the plane, rather than the pilot to him. He grudgingly put in a radio, which also meant having to maintain a battery, and for the next few seasons, the pilot didn't have to search him out. Karl only turned it on when he saw the plane land, and if the pilot had something for him, he would call "Conquest."

Long after we closed the air charter service, I got a call from a pilot who had brought a package from Karl back to Fort Lauderdale, with instructions to give it to me. Everyone was laughing when I arrived to see what Karl had sent. It was a small box. Inside was a note asking me to please get a tooth fixed in his upper plate, which was wrapped in a paper towel.

He included a $50 bill with the notation "I'm sure you can get this done quicker and for less money than sending to my wife."

Now at one time, we had brought Karl back to Fort Lauderdale for some emergency dental work, so, of course, he went to our dentist, who had also been to the island and was familiar with its primitive services. And, of course, we put him up during the time this work was being done, all for the price of his round trip from, and back to, the island. He assumed my dentist would be thrilled to take care of his current problem.

The note also said that he was not able to chew anything until his teeth returned, and that he really didn't like eating mush, so please hurry the process.

I took his upper teeth to my dentist, who, with a large grin, said, "You've got to be kidding me." I told him, "You know Karl." He explained that, without the bottom teeth, he really couldn't do a perfect job adding a tooth which had to meet another on the bottom jaw. I told him to give it a whirl.

A few days later, Karl's upper teeth were on their way back to the island with a little note from my dentist: "Whittle it to fit."

Drug Running

The late 1970s and early 1980s were a hot time in the Bahamas, which form a convenient corridor for drugs from South America, Jamaica, Haiti and other points of origin. Airplanes and boats routinely transported the substances to the U.S. via the islands. The Exumas, in particular, are still patrolled (sometimes at night without lights) by helicopter.

In those days, as now, it is only legal to land between sunup and sundown on airstrips without runway lights or control tower. Now, because aviation is such an integral part of tourism in the Bahamas and the number of private and commercial planes has dramatically increased, runway lights have been installed on all airstrips used by the public, available and turned on only for emergency.

Because we needed to talk to our own aircraft, we had installed a unicom radio at the Staniel Cay Yacht Club. We monitored 122.8, the frequency used by all pilots in uncontrolled airspace to report landings and take offs at all the little airstrips. Pilots could also call in to the club to order lunch, request transportation or rooms. The radio was on all the time, and was usually nothing more than background noise to those around the bar.

One very black night with no moon or stars, I heard a rather frantic voice with a Spanish accent on the unicom frequency. I answered the radio, asking for the plane's position. I got a panicked reply that he didn't know where he was. At that point, I told the pilot that I could hear him and to fly a pattern to stay where he was while we got vehicles to light up the runway. His voice kept getting higher, reporting he was very low on fuel.

Every available vehicle with lights was alerted to the airstrip. We had done this before, and everyone knew the drill. I stayed on the radio, but soon I could no longer hear the plane. The pilot was extremely upset and communication became more difficult as he slipped into Spanish more than English. Then there was no response. I had a horrible feeling that he didn't make it.

The next day the plane was spotted about ten miles off Norman's Cay. There were two bodies in the plane. Because it was packed full of marijuana bales, there was no way for the crew to get out even if they tried.

***

There were numerous drug busts at the island during the height of the doping days. I remember one in particular because I brought water and sodas several times to the DEA helicopter crew after they nabbed three Columbians and their airplane carrying about 400 pounds of cocaine, a huge quantity.

The helicopter was broken down, so they were waiting for another chopper to bring a mechanic and parts. In the meantime, the three Columbians were handcuffed in the hot sun. Although they claimed to only speak Spanish, the agents didn't believe them. The smugglers would have needed minimal knowledge of the language to venture into this part of the world, and English is required of all pilots.

So the agents started playing head games with the smugglers, talking as if they couldn't understand English. It's amazing what they understood when they overheard one of the agents say, "Let's just take them up and drop them overboard from about 5,000 feet...why clog the system with these low-lifes?" (or something to that affect.) It's amazing how fast they learned English.

***

I am including this next story to honor an innocent couple who were brutally murdered, probably by drug dealers, while cruising the Exumas on their sailboat in the summer of 1980. I am still outraged that this mystery was never solved and I firmly believe that someone alive today knows what happened. That person may be in jail for another crime or may have had an accomplice. I don't think someone could keep that big a secret for so many years without telling someone. There were errors in police work. Fear of touching the dead kept locals from retrieving the body when it was still in the dinghy. Because there were no bodies by the time the police finally reached the scene, and so much time lapsed before and after the boat was finally towed to Nassau, the case was closed for lack of evidence.

This is not a closed case. It is a cold case. So, Patty and William Kamerer of the sailing yacht *Kalia III* out of Fort

Myers, Florida, I am telling your story again on the slim chance that someone will come forward with the truth, even if it's almost 30 years later. You may have died, but your story is still alive and you are not forgotten.

***

On that fateful day, July 25, 1980. Trey was flying inbound to Staniel Cay to pick up passengers, and had his pilot friend, Bob, along for the ride. When he radioed his ETA for landing, he was asked to take a look at a boat at Pipe Cay, that a couple had been reported murdered and could Trey confirm that there was a body in the dinghy alongside a sailboat.

"Kenneth Rolle, of Staniel Cay, arrived in his boat about the same time I was circling," said Trey. "Bob took some photos with his new little spy-type camera and we could see the body wrapped in something blue in the dinghy. The *Kalia* looked like a ghost ship from the air."

Illinois State Representative Harry Yourell and his son Peter, the first on the grizzly scene, had radioed the information to Staniel Cay. When they arrived at the yacht club on their boat a short time later, they reported details of their gruesome findings so they could be conveyed to the authorities. They gave a description of the sailboat and how they found it, complete to blood smears, spent flare casings, the dinghy and the body. Kenneth returned to Staniel Cay shortly after, confirming the story, saying he had anchored the drifting sailboat but had left everything else the way it was because he didn't want to touch the dead body.

Yourell had taken photos, and gave the film to Trey to quickly get it developed in Fort Lauderdale. I put a rush on the film, which I remember as color slides. A day later, The couple's daughter and her husband came to our home from Fort Myers to view the slides on our projector. She was able to identify the body in the dinghy as her father, recognizing a mark on his neck. She also mentioned they had a cat onboard the boat, which Trey also recalls hearing about. No one knows what happened to the cat.

Trey took the slides back to Yourell, who was staying with his (and our) friend from Chicago who owned a house on Staniel Cay. As a photographer, I remember wanting to keep one of the slides or make copies, but they didn't belong to me. I can still see the slide show in my mind – what was once a beautiful boat, the dinghy, the body hanging over its side. Unfortunately, co-pilot Bob's photos, while recognizable, were taken at too great a distance from the air to convey the same detail of Yourell's excellent close-ups taken at the scene.

As a public relations writer, I knew this story was big, and as soon as Trey conveyed information on the radio from the island, I called the *Fort Lauderdale News* (now *Sun-Sentinel*) and told them if they wanted facts on the story they would soon be getting on the wires regarding a couple murdered aboard their sailboat in the Bahamas, to come see me, that I would give them the early, local findings, as well as information on the location. I wanted the focus on Pipe Cay, the scene of the crime, rather than on Staniel Cay, where reporters had to fly to cover the story.

When Trey flew over the next day, the body was no longer in the dinghy. No one knew what had happened. No one knew ANYTHING! Yet Rep. Yourell had reported the yacht was riddled with shotgun pellets, smeared with blood, and littered with debris, including Patty's eyeglasses and bikini top. It took more than a day for the police to arrive, and an early report from Nassau was that there had never been a body. They also denied there were shotgun holes in the yacht despite accounts from at least three witnesses. Yourell angrily made public the photos, proving there was a body in the dinghy and the condition of the sailboat. Bahamian authorities eventually admitted that a constable aboard a plane flying over the scene did spot the body and that the yacht was a shambles as Yourell had described. It was also confirmed that the U.S. Coast Guard had informed the Bahamian government that a 38-foot sailboat was missing. The occupants were author/electrician, William Kamerer, and his wife, Patty.

What happened to Patty, who was never seen or found? What happened to his body? Some say a shark could have grabbed it out of the dinghy. Perhaps the drug dealer turned killer returned in the dead of night and dumped it overboard to destroy evidence. It's still a mystery. But someone has to know the secret of what happened almost 30 years ago aboard *Kalia III*. It's not just another Bermuda Triangle tale. These were real, innocent people.

***

More detailed information, along with a theory on what probably happened, is online at http://www.bermuda-triangle.org/html/kalia_iii.html. I do not want to plagiarize a very well written and researched report. I merely want to keep their memory and the story alive.

Incidentally, the young reporter assigned the story at the *Fort Lauderdale News* eventually won an award for his excellent coverage of the incident.

***

At the time of the *Kalia* mishap, there was much talk about drug smuggling at Sampson Cay. New owners had taken over in the past couple of years, planes were landing on a rugged, short airstrip carved out on big Sampson Cay and mysterious boats came and left the dock at weird hours. All this took place prior to Marcus Mitchell acquiring Sampson Cay, including Little Sampson Cay, which was eventually sold to become the beautiful resort it is today. Marcus still owns part of Big Sampson, and has improved and expanded the original runway for his own use.

Shortly after the *Kalia* was towed to Nassau and everyone was acting like nothing happened, there was a ruckus involving the Sampson Cay alleged dopers and someone from Black Point, who may have wanted to blow the whistle on them.

It became a Keystone Cop shoot out. The Black Point person left Sampson Cay in his little boat being chased by the dopers, who followed him to Staniel Cay. They wielded their guns, took a few shots, and terrified all the residents and visitors at Staniel Cay. In those days, there was no policeman on the island as it had never been necessary. The natives protected the Black Point guy, hiding him from the shooters, who went door to door looking for him. He eventually made it home unscathed, but definitely shaken. No one was hurt, but the incident was talked about for years (in hushed tones so the tourists wouldn't hear).

Lobsters

The first Monday in August is Emancipation Day in the Bahamas, and it is the biggest holiday celebrated on Staniel Cay, more important than Independence Day, which is July 10th. Since the opening of lobster season is August 1, the holiday is a week-long event, celebrating the freeing of the slaves and capturing of the country's tastiest bounty of the sea.

Opening day meant scrambling to catch the most lobster in the shortest period of time, the equivalent of proving your manhood for the young men. In 1983, August Monday fell on Aug. 1, so the holiday was of mega proportions.

The yacht club employees had the day off, so we had to prepare our own meals. Family had come from all over to join us: Chamberlains, Hochers and Wohlfords. I was in the kitchen helping the women with the huge dinner. The men were doing what men do (bullshitting at the bar), and the boys were out getting the lobsters for dinner. Since not everyone liked the tasty bugs, we also had a couple of turkeys baking in the gas oven.

It was a big day for our boys, and everyone was excited and hoping for a good catch. They had armed themselves with

Hawaiian slings, with plenty of ice in coolers aboard the small Boston Whalers. You could feel the tension, the anticipation of hunters on opening day.

Late afternoon we saw the boys come in, all smiles with a great catch. We could see them cleaning the lobsters on the dock from inside the club.

Incidentally, the best way to "clean" a lobster is to break off one of its feelers (antennae) and twist it up into the lobster's back end...the barbs on the feeler attach to the innards and when you pull it out, the lobster is "clean." You then tear off the tail, save any fat legs for hors d'oeuvres, and it is ready for the pot. Ours was already boiling on the stove.

We waited for the boys to bring in dinner. The tables were set, everything was done but the lobster. We waited some more. Finally, we sent one of the men out to the dock to see what was the hold up.

There were NO LOBSTER tails!

The boys had taken an offer they couldn't refuse and had SOLD OUR DINNER on the dock to tourists!

Joe Hocher, dumbfounded, started lecturing the boys, then looked at Trey and me, and said "Let's go."

He and Trey grabbed snorkeling gear, slings from the boys, and the three of us hurriedly got in his boat. We headed toward the south end of Staniel Cay, where Joe claimed we'd find dinner. While I drove the boat, sometimes towing them to another location, Joe and Trey dove for lobsters, tossing them in the boat until we had enough for dinner. In a half-hour, we had a huge catch, which we cleaned on the way back to the yacht club. The bugs were tossed in the pot, and dinner was saved.

The boys ate rather quietly. Even though they had a few

bucks in their pockets, their catch had been trumped by the older generation. No lecture was needed and the adults pretty much ignored them. The next year, the boys did the hunting again, but this time, the catch made it to the table.

One of the exciting events of August Monday holiday is the Class C sailboat race from Staniel Cay to Black Point, five miles away, where there is also a huge celebration with a live band, lots of food and drink. These little cat-rigged sloops with such names such as *Termite*, *Slaughter*, *More Fire* and *Chaser*, have enormous gaff-rigged mainsails, loose footed on the boom. How hard the wind is blowing determines the number of crew. It's a delicate balance, because body weight is the ballast. One too many on board may lose the race because the boat is too heavy. One too few and the helmsman may have to keep dumping air to keep the boat from tipping over. When these little boats are perfectly balanced it is pure joy to watch them race.

Time

It's been years since Steve and Rita lived on the island. Enjoying God's heavenly reef, I still think of them every day.

At the annual island Christmas Eve party in 1985, when all the Americans and natives gathered at the old Chamberlain house for a feast and gift exchange, Steve and Rita gave us a hand-made clock – a straw fish mounted on wood. It hung in my Serenity cottage kitchen for years. When I tore down the cottage to build a new Serenity, I packed it away. When I unwrapped it, the clock mechanism was broken. I searched craft stores for one that would fit, to no avail. In the meantime, I hung the clock in my new kitchen. I soon realized that it shows exactly the right time all the time – Island Time. No hurry, Mon.

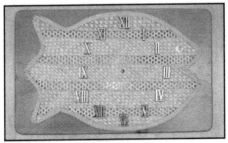

My kitchen clock from Steve and Rita.

Vehicles

With rocky paths as roads throughout much of the island, vehicles were always a problem. The early golf carts were gas driven and made of steel. Our first one was a Harley-Davidson. I have no idea what year it was, but they were made from 1967 to 1981. It began rusting from the time it arrived on Staniel Cay with its salty air and harsh environment.

Our next cart was a well-known brand, but it also rusted out rather quickly. Not until Club Car built carts with aluminum frames did they start to last, which also coincided with decent roads, more like paved paths, over much of the island. I still have electric Club Cars from 1987, 1992, 1996 and 2002. It's not easy or reasonable to keep them going, but I am managing and the frames are holding up. They've all seen better days.

Probably the most notorious vehicle of all time on Staniel Cay was Cyclops, so named for its one bright headlight mounted high on the front frame. Born as a jeep, Cyclops underwent so many changes, weldings and adaptations that it was hard to tell its lineage years later. There was one seat for the driver, which I believe may have come from a tractor.

Capt. Bob on one of the unusual island vehicles, a 3-wheeler.

The tires were always going flat on our rocky, unpaved roads, so a scuba tank was carried to fill the tires along the way, which was never very far. The only place it went was about a half-mile in either direction, to the dump or to the airstrip from the yacht club. It was painted fire engine red, probably to blend with all the rust.

Another peculiarity was the gas tank. The original one rusted out long before I arrived, so I only saw a portable out-board boat tank lashed to the frame. It was easily taken off and filled at the island's only pump on the yacht club dock.

This amazing one-eyed contraption, with a wood box built onto its back and benches along both sides, was the orig-inal Staniel Cay taxi. It moaned and groaned as the driver shifted gears, but somehow got people from Point A to Point

B as long as no one minded a few squirts of air in the tires along the way or a cough or sputter which made a few loud backfires.

While Cyclops was nearing the end of its usefulness and a more conventional vehicle was needed to transport people between the yacht club and airstrip, a VW bus, perhaps the original, arrived on the island. I have no idea who found this for the yacht club or how it got to the island. The insides were gutted, so wood seats were crudely built in. The whole vehicle was painted a milky beige inside and out, and when the door was closed, it was like a furnace inside, especially during summer.

I don't know if the engine was much better than the one in Cyclops, because the VW bus did not last very long. One of the local boys (I won't say who) accidentally drove it off the government dock into the salt water one day as the weekly freight boat arrived from Nassau. By the time they pulled it onto the little beach and back on to the road it was never the same.

Old Sea Captains

Skeeze is one of the funniest people I've ever met. He can convincingly tell a story with twists and turns and you never know if you should believe him or not.

One fall, which was off-season at the Staniel Cay Yacht Club, a visitor and his wife arrived in their own plane with, of all things, an inflatable boat. He was a writer, doing a story on fast-track cruising the Bahamas by plane using the rubber boat wherever they landed to snorkel and explore the sites. We watched him hand-pump his boat, attach the small outboard, and push it in the water off the public beach.

Skeeze decided the writer had to have a better story, and when he came into the club for lunch, began chiding him about his rubber toy, that it was hardly "cruising," and that he was wondering how he ended up at this rest home reserved for whacked out yacht captains during the off season.

At first the man ignored him, but in Skeeze's style, he talked to us just loud enough to get his attention. The writer finally asked a few questions about retired yacht captains, and Skeeze explained, elaborating on everyone he saw at the club.

"Captain Bob, there, he thinks he's running the place, but

he's in charge of shaking everyone's hand and smiling like the colonel (Sanders) he resembles. He used to be captain of the *Malabar* until he went a little crazy and deaf. He still thinks she's docked outside and that guests will be arriving any minute for a charter."

Bob, not hearing what Skeeze was saying but seeing that we were all smiling and looking at him, smiled back from ear to ear, nodding his head as if in agreement. He turned to Joe Hocher standing next to him and said, "It's a fine day for sailing. Just the right breeze. Too bad the boats aren't here."

Skeeze then talked about Capt. Joe, a former truck driver, and how he had come to the island on a 19-foot boat from Chicago years ago in the hopes of taking people diving.

"Yep," said Skeeze. "He loves to dive, but his real expertise is underwater demolition, so we have to keep an eye on him. He loves to blow up things. Just the other day, someone needed rock cleared for a foundation of a house. He damn near blew up the whole island. Rocks flew everywhere. He can't figure how much of the stuff to use on land to get the job done. Still calculates like he's working under water. Don't worry, though, I think he used up the last of the dangerous stuff."

The writer, still skeptical, pointed to Trey.

"What's his story?"

Skeeze and Trey started to laugh and we girls were giggling over what he would say about Trey.

"Well, he started out as a yacht captain, and was pretty successful until he burned out. Threw everyone off the boat and told them to swim home. Then he decided to start flying planes. I'm sure you saw that red and white bird next to yours?" The writer nodded.

"If you look more closely at it, you'll see that it has propellers, but no engines. It's for his own good, as no one thinks he should still fly. We've got it rigged with huge rubber bands so we can wind up the props, he can sit in the cockpit, and think he's getting ready to take off," he said, dead-pan serious. "He doesn't even know what I'm saying right now because his brain is fried from too much rum."

Trey lifted his glass in a toast to Skeeze.

"And you?" the writer asked?

Trey said, "I know that one!"

And this one was true.

"We met Skeeze and Maggie right after they bought their charter boat," he began. "We had just sold our sailboat and gotten out of the charter business. Marty was assigned to do a PR story on them, so we were invited to their kick-off captain's cocktail party in Fort Lauderdale."

When Trey found out they planned to operate in the Bahamas, he cautioned them about all the trials and tribulations of chartering, how some people are wonderful, but others are demanding and unappreciative.

"I told them their boat looks great dockside, but just wait until they finish a season of chartering. They'd be lucky to recognize it. Now after a few years being at the whim and call of all sorts of people who thought their yacht was a hotel, Skeeze and Maggie are here on a little houseboat trying to find what he was supposed to show his guests. He mostly sits right here drinking rum and Coke."

At this point, Harry walked in, and we all looked at Skeeze for another story.

"That guy who just walked in? Well, he's a retired yacht captain also. He had his boat tied to the docks out there during a tropical storm a couple of years ago. It was so bad the conch shells were landing inside the bar when the wind took the door off. Everyone told him to take it to safe anchorage, but he said, 'Nah, she'll ride it out.' By the time the storm hit he couldn't physically get off the boat tied between all the pilings because it was rocking so bad. As he ran out of rum, someone at the bar would put on a foul weather jacket and battle the wind out to his boat and toss another bottle along with a sandwich. The boat rocked so hard it mixed up his head forever. We would see Harry leaning to one side, then the other. Now he just LOOKS at a moving boat and gets vertigo."

Harry waved, his eyes twinkling as he grinned. He had no idea what Skeeze had just said about him.

That afternoon we went to Osprey Cay to enjoy the pristine beach, collect shells, swim, and just enjoy an outing with the kids. We took three Boston Whalers so everyone would have room for beach towels and sand toys. After a nice swim and watching the kids build castles, we headed back to Staniel Cay. One boat ran out of gas, so another took it in tow. When we arrived at the yacht club, the writer and his wife looked at the scene and shook their heads.

Skeeze looked up at him.

"Guess we can't even remember to put gas in a boat anymore."

A few months later, we heard someone say they had read an article written by a guy flying the Bahamas packing a rubber dinghy. They said it mentioned a professional captain in a little boat at Staniel Cay being towed by another professional captain in a little boat because he had run out of gas. It cautioned people to investigate a yacht and its crew before sending a deposit for a charter.

Capt. Bob

There are many stories that can be told about Capt. Bob Chamberlain. He was the perfect greeter for anyone coming to the yacht club, a fixture that everyone looked forward to meeting.

Long before we began our air charter service to the island, Bob had a four-seat single engine Cessna that would land and take off on the original, short, gravel runway. He mostly used the plane for the family and to go to Nassau for supplies, but occasionally he would take paying guests, even though he was not a commercial pilot. Back then, people got where they wanted to any way they could, and Capt. Bob was always willing to fly, which he loved almost as much as being captain of his beloved retired schooner *Malabar*.

One time, flying into Nassau, he identified himself as "TWA" on the radio. Someone overheard and asked if TWA was now flying to the Bahamas.

Bob replied that TWA had been flying between Nassau and Staniel Cay for some years, but that it wasn't widely advertised.

The other pilot asked what type of aircraft they were

using, knowing the primitive conditions of the runway at the island, which was flagged as "private" on all the charts to discourage anyone from landing.

Bob said, "Well, as you know, it would have to be small. I'm flying a Cessna 172."

There was a long silence.

"And you did say TWA?" the other pilot asked.

"That's a roger," Capt. Bob replied. "Teeny Weeny Airlines."

From that point on the word was out. TWA did indeed fly to Staniel Cay.

Another story involves Capt. Bob often being mistaken for Col. Sanders of chicken fame. One time he arrived in Nassau, and a tourist came up to him, saying "Col. Sanders, may I have your autograph?"

Bob smiled, took a piece of paper, listened to her expound on how good his chicken was, wrote a little note and handed it to her with his signature.

He told her to take it to Col. Sanders downtown Nassau, that it was good for a free dinner on him.

As the real "colonel" had been dead for some years, I am not sure what happened when she showed up with the note.

Big Bird

One morning in the early 1980s, Lucille, a retired American lady who lived on South Staniel, came into the yacht club and excitedly reported there were footprints on the beach that had to belong to an enormous bird or some unknown creature. She said they followed the shoreline along South Staniel's large horseshoe beach, then disappeared into the shallow water.

After accusing her of "seeing things," several of the locals went to investigate before the tide rose. Sure enough, there was evidence that some huge creature with feet about twelve inches in diameter had walked the beach at low tide, then entered the water. Young kids looked bug-eyed at the evidence, and began conjuring up what this creature must look like. Imaginations went wild, and of course, it became the main topic of conversation on the island, fueled by Lucille's insistence she wasn't "crazy."

Much talk evolved as to what this could possibly be, and then some other people reported hearing a very weird sound, like a huge bird squawk, in the early morning before sunrise. Lucille, who occasionally tended bar at the yacht club, swore the creature was real, and expressed fear of it attacking her or one of the kids. After a few rum punches, anything was possible with this creature, which by now was estimated to be at least five feet tall with a wingspan of enormous proportions. As no one had seen it, speculation was that it must be nocturnal and only flew to the island during the night. The kids went on a hunt looking for a huge nest, thinking that's why it probably returned, but found nothing.

After about two weeks, the footprints appeared less and less, and it was believed that whatever it was may finally have gone elsewhere, but speculation continued, fueled by Lucille's insistence that this creature did, indeed exist, and that her eyesight was still good.

About a month later, a package arrived at the yacht club. When it was opened, it showed a picture of Russell Ott in a white tuxedo sipping champaign, wearing the "big bird" feet. A frequent visitor to the island, he and his family often rented a house on South Staniel and was there during the Big Bird event. When Lucille saw the picture, she was outraged that he had pulled a fast one on her. She carried on for days, mad as can be, with everyone teasing her and howling with laughter every time they looked at the picture behind the yacht club bar. You'd have to know Lucille to get the full impact. Everyone loved her, but knew she could be gullible. I don't think she ever forgave Russ.

The picture hung in the bar for several years, so the story was told again and again, embellished with rum punches and achieving a life of its own. The kids, of course, swore they knew it was a joke all along.

Mary Lou

From 1993 to 2005, the island was blessed to have a full-time nurse from the States, Mary Lou Fadden. Her tireless devotion to the island will long be remembered.

A series of events led up to her coming to the island. She and husband Glen had sailed to Staniel Cay in 1991 and through knowing several people in the Staniel Cay area, were put in touch with Donna Chamberlain and Steve Smith, whom they had never met, about providing nursing care at the island. St. Luke's Clinic was originally begun by Donna Chamberlain and Ann Hocher, and was a private, not government facility, so until recently, Staniel Cay did not have a government nurse.

In accepting the position, Mary Lou knew it was strictly on a volunteer basis. Never did she imagine she'd be seeing thousands of people each year as word spread of her skills, tireless devotion and professional manner. But before she arrived, everything had to be put in order.

"There was nothing in the clinic that could be used," she said. "It was basically empty except for the termites, rats and needles. The apartment wasn't finished, yet that's where we stayed."

In the States, friends and home owners at Staniel Cay collected medical supplies. The Faddens bought some things with their own money because they were told there was lots of money in the bank. It turned out to be only $147.00! Money from checks that had gone to other accounts eventually did make it back into the account, but it was an initial shock.

Nurse Mary Lou and husband Glen.

No matter what time or weather conditions, Mary Lou was always ready to go when called. Her only fear was that she wouldn't be able to get to someone in time.

I asked Glen how he felt about all the work she did.

"It was amazing to me to watch some of the procedures she performed," he said. "I finally started asking myself 'where did she learn that?' I would then come to whatever conclusion fit. Her time working for a dentist, or this hospital, that hospital, etc. So much of what she did was a team effort for us. When she was called out to a patient, my job was to fire up the generator, get the lights and air conditioning on, and have the clinic ready for her arrival."

One holiday she was taken by boat to Cistern Cay to attend to a kid who had been injured with a cutlass.

"It was a rough ride. His back looked like a big 'Z' with cuts. He said he had fallen on the cutlass, not saying who did it to him," she said. "We got him on a plane that was waiting at Norman's Cay and he went right to Nassau. They never did prosecute anyone."

There were shark bites, barracuda bites, heart attacks, human attacks, construction accidents, and everyday blood pressure and routine checks for everyone in the village. Boaters needing medical help would speed to Staniel Cay so she could treat them. She could stitch a wound more professionally than some doctors. Every incident was documented, and she kept charts on everyone she treated.

The big problem was when something happened at night, as runway lights for emergency landings weren't installed until after she left the island.

"I've sat up all night with someone praying their appendix wouldn't burst or something worse happen," she said.

When Kenneth and Theaziel Rolle had medical problems in their old age, she provided hospice care, visiting four or more times a day.

"Like most people, the natives never think they're going to die tomorrow, even after a diagnosis of cancer or other fatal disease," she said. "Some, such as Rev. Kelly and Mama Di, were the picture of health, then suddenly gone. On a small island where everyone is family, it gets to you."

She had to pronounce many a visitor or resident dead, writing out death certificates and sometimes riding with an officer to Nassau for a body to be autopsied.

"Even if death was expected, bodies still had to be autopsied," she said.

She has no idea how many times she was called out in the night.

"People never knew what my job entailed," she said. "One guy knocked on the door in the middle of the night and told Glen to get me up, that he had to see me right away. His problem could have waited until morning, but I treated him. Several times in the night men came wanting condoms. Glen would tell them they should have thought of them earlier. Eventually we brought some upstairs to the apartment so we could just hand them out as needed."

I asked if she ever thought she was taken for granted.

"Absolutely," she said. "I didn't let it get me down because my mission was much bigger than that. I stayed because it was what the Lord wanted me to do."

Cat Tales

In the mid-1990s, I helped solve my rat problem by welcoming a feral island cat, Tootsie, to Serenity cottage. I had returned for a couple weeks of vacation and found her under the cottage with a litter of three kittens.

While Tootsie mainly hung out at Club Thunderball, her offspring stayed at the cottage. Splash was the only female in that first litter, and she began to mass-produce kittens. To feed the growing population, I sent bags of cat food with my guests from the States. I figured it was cheap rodent control. The cats and kittens never came inside, and were a great source of amusement to my guests, especially children.

Splash was special. If a mama cat somehow disappeared and left her babies, Splash would nurse them. Some kittens would be attacked by aggressive soldier hermit crabs, who would bite an ear or tail of a baby kitten, maiming it for life. Many didn't survive the harsh environment.

While cats are not as prolific as, say, rabbits, Serenity soon had a consistent population of about a dozen adult cats. The more aggressive males were chased away or taken off the island, the best I could do on birth control. We had no veterinarian and I certainly wasn't going to pay for them to get neutered in Nassau, even if I could catch them. The problem was eventually solved by someone who, I understand, put a bounty on the stray cats. I don't want to know what happened to them. It was off-season and the cats had to fend for themselves.

When I returned late November, only one cat crawled out of the bush to greet me – my favorite Splash. She let me pick her up. I brought her into the cottage, where I began the taming process, and eventually brought her to the States, where she was spayed, aborted and de-clawed the first day. She lived in Fort Lauderdale while the new Serenity was built, and was eventually brought back to the island, where she continues to keep me company along with Kitta, another rescued cat from my old neighborhood.

Her story is told in a children's book I wrote, *Splash - The Staniel Cay Cat*, illustrated by local artist Bernadette Chamberlain.

Your Mission, Should you Accept...

Over the years I developed a reputation as an expeditor. If a part was needed for a boat, we'd find it. If someone needed to get somewhere once we got them off the island, we arranged tickets to their destination. Everyone in our office took the word "service" seriously. In a 1983 magazine article on the island, Trey and I were referred to as the "life line" and principal link for the island. In time, these connections grew, and calls came from a variety of sources requesting services. Here are some that I remember.

Request: Each charter week supply a 56-foot trimaran with groceries to arrive on the same flight as its passengers to Staniel Cay.

The only way to know how many mouths to feed was to check the flight manifest, then add three more for the crew.

I never got a list of what they needed or wanted, but in time, I was able to go to the grocery store, fill two carts with enough food for a week, ten days or two weeks, for as many people onboard during that time period.

At first it was daunting, but I mentally created menus as I walked the grocery aisles, envisioning what sides went with what entrees, realizing that the person on the receiving end may mix things up entirely. I just knew to ship enough food for three squares a day within the alloted budget.

It got to be a game, because every week I'd include a surprise: strawberries with whipped cream; some exotic fruit in season on the other side of the world; a bouquet of fresh cut flowers; a birthday or anniversary cake if I knew someone was celebrating...and if I REALLY wanted to impress them, ice cream packed in a cooler with dry ice. Before the freight boats had freezers, ice cream was the most exotic treat you could have on the island. If we had space on the plane, we'd send ice cream on dry ice to the yacht club to serve as dessert. Often, it disappeared before dinner.

Request: Send a replacement diesel engine for a Morgan 42 sailboat to replace one blown by bareboat charter party on Wednesday, to be delivered and installed for next charter on Saturday. Also send mechanics to install.

We were handling bookings for this boat, so knew the schedule and had contact with each charter party and, we thought, thoroughly checked the experience of anyone we allowed aboard. This particular one must have had too many rum punches. He ran the diesel engine without checking the oil, and when it ran out, the engine seized. It was a Wednesday when the boat was towed into the yacht club, and I was notified to cancel the next charter as the boat needed a new engine.

We told the charter party who blew the engine to get

themselves and all their personal gear off the boat.

Instead of cancelling the next group, I started calling my sources to locate a diesel engine that would fit the boat. I went to Joe, owner of an engine service in Fort Lauderdale who had bailed us out time and again when we needed something for our own boat in the past. He just happened to have the right engine sitting in his shop. I explained the situation, and with a big smile, he said, "We can do this." I didn't have the $4,000 or whatever the cost was, but he said don't worry, "We can do this." I radioed the club to get the old engine out of the boat, that we were NOT missing a charter. There was a davit on the dock, and with the muscle of a few volunteers, they were able to hoist it out of the boat, no easy chore on a sailing vessel, which typically has a very small, hard-to-reach engine compartment. It was a SAILboat, after all. Engines were secondary back then.

On Thursday, the new engine was loaded on our plane with a forklift along with two mechanics and all the necessary fittings and hoses. By the time the plane landed, the boat was ready for the new engine, again a feat of muscle and ingenuity to not only get the engine off the plane into whatever vehicle was running at the time, but to install it in the narrow engine compartment of the sailboat. The mechanics worked all day Thursday and all day Friday while I stayed in communication and bit my nails in Fort Lauderdale. I did NOT want to call the next charter party to tell them we didn't have a boat for them.

Friday night they radioed it was done. Everyone celebrated except the charter party who had caused the problem. Saturday morning the next group arrived and received careful instructions on breaking in the new engine.

When I took him payment, Joe admitted he couldn't have done the job faster in Fort Lauderdale. He beamed when he said, "We DID it!"

Request: Handle a semi-trailer truck full of goods originating in Philadelphia scheduled to arrive in Miami, to a grass airstrip on Crooked Island, along with numerous other items (list attached) needed to open a resort. You are to secure a suitable aircraft for the job and arrange clearing of goods through Bahamian Customs, which includes handling payment of duty on the cargo.

About 1978, a man returning from Staniel Cay asked to meet with us. Since our office was in our home at the time, we invited him over. He explained that he headed a group of investors who wanted to create a resort similar to the yacht club at another location in the Bahamas. I handed him a copy of Herman Wouk's *Don't Stop the Carnival*, told him to read it and rethink his plan.

About a month later he returned for another meeting. He handed me the book and said, "It's not funny. We still want to do it, and we've decided where."

He explained that his group of ten investors, all professionals, had just purchased an abandoned resort on Crooked Island, which is almost two hundred miles further south than Staniel Cay. We listened, believing he was truly rock happy before his time. We explained the logistics in getting people to the resort, the difficulty of communications, the uncertainty of getting supplies that far south. He didn't want to hear anything negative. What was done was done. He spread out his plans and began outlining his dream.

We flew to Pittstown Point Landings in our small twin-engine Navajo, bringing in some of the supplies he requested. He had told us the airstrip was rough and only about 2,000 feet long. Once we landed, riding the dips in the soft terrain, we knew we would have to be extremely light to take off. We mentally calculated that we could not transport people unless major improvements were done to the airstrip. The marginal conditions also complicated the challenge to fly in everything to rebuild, refurbish, and create the resort atmosphere they envisioned.

We began calling to see how it could happen. In researching aircraft, one in particular seemed to fit all the criteria for landing and taking off on the small airstrip and which could also carry the heavy loads. I refer to the Caribou we found in Miami as a "mini Herk." It was a 72-foot long twin-engine plane with big tires, capable of taking off and landing in less than 1,000 feet with a wing span over 90 feet. The Caribou was primarily a military aircraft designed to carry 32 troops or a quarter ton truck. When we looked it over, everything in the plane was labeled in both English and Vietnamese. The rear cargo door dropped to became a ramp, making loading

The Caribou over Staniel Cay on its way south.

and unloading very easy. The plane was strictly utilitarian and slow, with a speed of less than 150 knots per hour.

We got the price and figured we'd need at least three flights to transport what was already building in a warehouse. In addition to all the bedding, appliances, kitchen supplies, a custom stainless steel stove hood to suit the hotel guidelines of the Bahamas, we also had to bring in shower doors, building supplies, dive tanks and related equipment, plus deck furniture – the list grew every day.

I found myself driving all over south Florida for miscellaneous cargo they kept ordering.

One day I was headed over the 17th Street Bridge for yet more gear for Pittstown, and had to wait for a very long bridge opening. A policeman on a motorcycle came alongside my little Fiat Spider and motioned for me to roll down my window. He pointed out that my license plate was out of date. I explained to him that I had received my new sticker, but it was on the mantle of my fireplace behind a stack of windows that had arrived for the house we were remodeling, and that I'd be sure to have them moved so I could reach it and put it on. Then he asked to see the vehicle inspection, because back then, every car had to be inspected each year. I rummaged through my glove box and handed him the only inspection report I had. He said, "This is also expired." Then he asked for my license, and at this point, I started giggling. He said, "No." I said "Yes." He said, "Lady, one item I can warn you about, two items I might let slide, but THREE out of date? I've got to give you a ticket." So in the next two weeks I also got my car squared away, went to court, and watched the judge's face as he tried not to grin. After paying a small fine, I was again in the good graces of the State of

Florida.

The Pittstown project was a logistics nightmare. I prepared the manifest, listing everything that was to be shipped, its weight, its value, its category for duty. When it came time for the first flight, I said the engineer's seat had my name on it. What a thrill! The plane was so noisy I had to communicate with the pilot and co-pilot with headphones, even though I could touch each of them. The plane was so slow we could actually fly with the side cockpit windows open, a blessing since the plane did not have air conditioning.

As we approached the famous Bird Island lighthouse, built on Castle Rock in 1876 just off Pittstown, we could see the landing strip. I can't describe the knot in my stomach as we came to land that huge bird on that little strip of grass. It was not the first time in for me, but it was for the pilots. They circled before landing to get a feel for it, then came in off the water and put those big tires on the grass with hardly a bump. I looked behind me and saw that everything packed to the ceiling was just as secure as when we took off.

Several of the investors were on the island awaiting the arrival of the cargo, and everyone came out to meet the plane. It was like Christmas. What a celebration!

The next few hours were spent unloading the aircraft so it could head back to Miami for the next day's load.

On one of the flights, the weather socked in prior to landing, and the crew opted to land at Colonel Hill, the main runway for Crooked Island that was 3,500 feet long and paved. Unfortunately, the road between Colonel Hill and Pittstown, or nearby Landrail Point, was not. There was more hassle moving the cargo 20 miles over a rutted, rocky road with all available (old) vehicles, than in transporting it all from the States.

Request: Relocate 5,000 pounds of unspecified goods that included items 20 feet long from Bermuda to some port on the East Coast, to be determined the day of the flight.

The first call I got was on a Friday morning from some-one in a Fortune 500 company in their New Jersey office. They explained what they needed, but not what the cargo was, and asked if I could do the job. I told them I'd try and would get back to them within an hour or so. They said that would be great, as everyone they had asked so far said it couldn't be done except in a jet aircraft which was beyond their budget for this particular project.

It didn't take long for me to realize the complexity of moving 5,000 pounds spanning 20 feet a distance of over 1,000 miles. I soon accumulated facts. There was no aviation fuel available in Bermuda at that time, only Jet A fuel, which is why others had said it could only be done in a jet. Because Bermuda is so far from the mainland, any aircraft flying there had to be equipped with "long-wire" radio as there were no NDBs (non directional beacons) for navigation. Long-wire, or single-sideband radiotelephony first became common in the 1930s, and was used extensively for communications to ships and aircraft over water. It was not common in aircraft at the time this flight was to be made. Another fact was that we had to receive permission (I can't remember the Washington agency) to make the flight.

I began calling every freight charter operation in the Southeast. When I finally reached Seagreen Transport in Miami, I started to have hope. Yes, they had an aircraft that could do the job. Yes, it could go round trip and would not need to refuel in Bermuda. Yes, it was available that night.

Yes, it was equipped with long-wire radio. Yes, they could tell me who to call to get permission to do the flight. Just make sure all the money was wired prior to take-off.

It was already 2 p.m. and the flight was to depart Miami at 1 a.m. I called the company, gave them the necessary information, along with wiring information for my bank. They said they would do it. I called the guys at Seagreen and told them it was a go. At 5 p.m. I got a call from the company. Because of its size, the requisition for the money had to go through a number of channels and they couldn't do it on such short notice. I told them it was a no-go without funds, and cancelled the trip.

Two weeks later, they called and said they were ready to wire the money if I could again put the charter together. They sheepishly told me I was the only one who had told them it could be done at that price. They wanted a 7:30 a.m. pick up in Bermuda. I immediately called Seagreen and it was set up for 1 a.m. that night. I told them part of the deal was that I went with them. They tried to talk me out of it (no heat in the plane, it was old, not pretty, there was no head aboard, yada, yada, yada). I told them I'd bring my winter jacket, hat and gloves, empty my bladder before stepping aboard and I didn't care if the plane was pretty or not, as long as the engines were in good shape, which they assured me they were. As a private pilot, I was NOT going to miss this opportunity. I met the three pilots at midnight at a Denny's near Miami International and we drove to their base at the airport. Looking back, I was very trusting, not knowing any of them prior to that night, and willing to fly to a little dot in the Atlantic Ocean with no communication back home. Herbie, the captain, assured me they were okay guys and they didn't mind me coming along since I was a pilot.

I was not mentally prepared for the sight of this plane. It was a huge DC-4, with four large round engines with a tall ladder propped against an open cargo door for getting aboard.

As I climbed up, I looked inside the plane. It was huge, gutted to the outside panels, with rollers along the floor for moving cargo. Herbie told me to sit in a jump seat behind the copilot, and the crew of three took their places – pilot, co-pilot and engineer. As he cranked over the first engine, the roar gave me a thrill, multiplied as the other three engines started turning those huge four-bladed propellers. It was like I was on a ride at Disney World. We all had headsets to communicate, because the noise was deafening. As we took off, I glanced behind me at the huge empty cavern. I had pulled it off! We were on our way to Bermuda, approximately six-and-a-half hours away.

It was cold. I had taken precaution to not drink anything a few hours prior to boarding. After the first half-hour, it was pretty boring, and I felt myself doze on and off. I think the pilots took turns napping also, because I saw Herbie's head bob time and again.

It was eerie as dawn broke. Gradually, the sky lightened, until a burst of sun announced the day. Herbie told me we were right on time. Soon I heard him talking to the tower and we were preparing to land.

We were greeted by company personnel who had arranged the charter and were whisked off to clear customs and immigration, and to have our papers stamped and signed for the return flight. It would be to Wilmington, North Carolina, where we would be met by more company personnel. By the time I used the restroom and returned to the plane, the cargo was loaded, all wrapped up in white plastic and unidentifiable. I couldn't imagine what we were carrying that was so important and yet so secret.

The flight back was incredible. Herbie actually let me fly the plane for seven hours! It was basic instruments, nothing fancy, like flying a little two-seater trainer but at dinosaur proportions. I don't think I stopped smiling the whole way back. I knew Herbie was the "real" pilot, but just being at the controls was thrilling.

Flying in the DC-4.

As we approached Wilmington, Herbie took the left pilot seat and I went to my jump seat. When we landed, there were several company personnel on hand to congratulate and thank me. I finally had to ask. What were we carrying?

One man smiled and explained.

With relations with Cuba the way they were, almost all the phone lines between Key West and the island had deteriorated. Because new technology equipment could not be installed, they had to use what was available, and the only equipment that was relatively in good shape was what we had carried out of Bermuda. It was going to be loaded on a ship bound for Key West and beyond.

The next day I bought a wall unit for our television room with the profits of the charter.

About 15 years later, I was taking my mother to Staniel Cay on a chartered twin-engine Aztec out of Fort Lauderdale International. I rode co-pilot. Along the way, I kept looking at the pilot, and he kept glancing my way. He was humming, which was a bit annoying, until I remembered that hum way back in my subconscious. Simultaneously, the pilot looked at me and me at him and we both said "Bermuda!" Herbie was our pilot. The rest of the trip we reminisced. Seagreen Transport had long ago closed its doors and Herbie was back piloting small airplanes. It didn't matter. What was important was that he was still flying.

Mother Blanche

Born November 9, 1892 on Farmer's Cay, a settlement about 18 miles south of Staniel Cay, Blanche H. Gray married Richard Gray in 1917 in Nassau, whose father had founded the settlement of Staniel Cay in the late 1800s. Her husband earned his living fishing and farming, and Blanche became a mid-wife, had six children or her own, and helped raised many grandchildren. She was the island disciplinarian, and any child, whether native or visitor, listened to her loving guidance. They were often treated to her homemade peppermint candy.

Tourists visiting the island sought the wisdom of "Ma Blanche" or just "Mama" as she was known throughout the Exumas, the peaceful, lovable matriarch of Staniel Cay.

She was often referred to as the island's "chamber of commerce." She set the example in etiquette and ethics. She looked after everyone's welfare, and if someone was hungry or without clothes, she fed and clothed them. She was a living example of the Golden Rule.

Every time we arrived with our children, the first thing they did was pay their respects to Mother Blanche. If they forgot, we would send them to her house in the village to begin their vacation again.

One summer, when daughter Coral was bored, she joined the native women at the Gray house and learned how to plat palm tops that would eventually become straw bags and mats in Nassau.

Mama took an active role in church activities at Mount Olivet Baptist Church, and every Sunday, she would sit in the front pew.

In 1973, the second freight boat to the island was named the *Lady Blanche* in her honor.

Because I personally had such respect and love for her, I vowed that no matter the circumstances, I would attend her funeral, or "home-going." When she died in the heat of summer on July 31, 1991, there was no air service at the time from Fort Lauderdale to the island. The day before her funeral

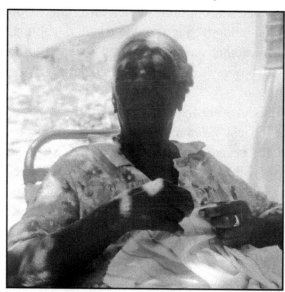

Mother Blanche.

was scheduled I was still trying to figure a way to the island. I was eventually advised to call one of her sons, Lenneth Brozozog in Nassau, who told me to board *The Grand Master* at Potter's Cay Dock in Nassau by 11 a.m. on Friday, the day before her funeral at Staniel Cay. I arrived, and family members welcomed me aboard.

The vessel was captained by her son, Capt. Rolly Gray. Although his normal freight run was from Nassau to Georgetown, this time he was taking his mother home for the last time. The hearse arrived, and everyone gathered as the casket was loaded on the boat. At about 1:30 we departed Potter's Cay for the Exumas. The mood was joyful. The women set their hair, everyone chatted, happy to be with so much family, and children played. Capt. Rolly was at the helm.

At one point, someone said, "See that boat listing to the side? See how no one is on this side? Watch as we pass." Through the rough deck openings we could see solid bodies packed aboard the Haitian vessel bound for Nassau.

We watched the sun set into the sea, a gorgeous yellow and pink sunset to bless our voyage.

About a half hour out from Staniel Cay, everyone began to sing hymns. I asked someone what was happening. I was told they were "singing the body in." It was so solemn, so beautiful, so reverent for her arrival on the island, where everyone lined the dock waiting for us. It was then that I noticed I was the only American aboard. What a privilege to be with the family!

The wake went all night, with everyone coming and going, singing, greeting one another..."Oh what a glory..." The drums and tambourines kept the beat to guitars and voices. Someone directed the singing while people came in to sign the guest book and view "Mother" for the last time.

There were so many people on the island, well over 500, that they had to sleep in shifts. Because I had guests in my Serenity cottage, I was invited to stay with Vivian and Berkie in their home along with many, many relatives.

When it came time for the actual funeral service, all the men wore black and the women wore white. It was a time for family portraits, and one group after another posed under the almond tree in the Gray family yard in front of the church. Kenneth Rolle, one of her sons, wore a formal black top hat for the occasion.

The photo session took some time to record and document so many family members. Everyone filed into the church for her final home-going celebration: children and parents, aunts and uncles, grandchildren, great-grandchildren, nieces and nephews.

Rev. Alpheus Kelly led the service. Government dignitaries and long time friends joined the family. When it was over, the procession stretched from the church to the village cemetery, voices lifted in song..."I will meet you in the morning....over there."

It was a sweltering hot day, but no one seemed to mind. It was Mother's home-going.

At her death, she left 37 grandchildren, 73 great-grandchildren and 16 great-great-grandchildren. Her legacy lives on in the many smiling island faces.

***

On Feb. 17, 2008, the Grand Master, Capt. Rolly Gray, passed at the age of 85, a Bahamian legend. I am including

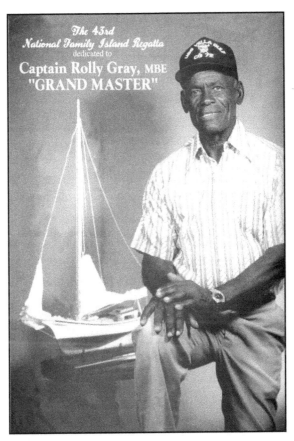

Rolly Gray portrayed in annual regatta program.

details of this man's life because it is a testimony to his legacy and the island of Staniel Cay. It's the character of these two individuals that qualify why people fall in love with the island, and why I have stayed. The following is the tribute from his son, Capt. Tony Gray, at his funeral.

Rolly Bertram Gray was born at Gray Cay (now called Staniel Cay), Exumas, Bahamas, on Tuesday, 22nd August, 1922.

He was fortunate to have lived in the ancient and modern Bahamas.

During his early years as a young teen, he fell in love with the sea and chose fishing as his career. It was not an easy one, for hardship was the order of the day, but a man as he was with a brave heart. He pressed on knowing that there was little or no other choice in which to make a living.

During his more than thirty years as a fisherman, he frequently supplied Her Majesty's Prison and other fish vendors in New Providence with his catch of the day.

Many other fishermen admired his skills and highly respected him as one of the best during that time.

The ancient way of fishing was a tough and rough one. Fishermen at that time used sailing vessels called smack boats. They used small dinghies with sculling oars. They had no motors. They had no refrigeration, They had to eat fresh sea food or dry fish or conch after hanging them out to dry in the sun.

When it was bedtime, some fishermen didn't know whether they were going to sleep in a wet or dry bed, because many of the vessels sometimes leaked from the deck with either rain or sea water.

My father went through those hard times without any complaint, just to take it as it was during the decade of the late 1960s. As the Bahamas was being transformed into a more modern country, my father decided to abandon his fishing career and start a new one. In 1968, he entered the mail boat service. He wanted to make a better way of life and be in a better position to serve the people and help build the Exumas.

From 1968 to 2004, during his more than three decades in that service, he was the Senior Master of three mail boats, namely *Staniel Cay Express*, *Lady Blanche* and *The Grand Master*. The mail boat service was not an easy one either, especially in the early years when you had to lift every single thing by hand.

As Senior Master, my father worked more than hard. He spent many hours at the helm and many sleepless nights travelling from one port to another on a weekly basis year after year.

As Senior Master on those mailboats, the following is a rough estimate of miles and hours logged during his time.

• *Staniel Cay Express* service between New Providence and Exuma Cays from April 1968 to November 1975: 97,270 miles and 9,727 hours.

• *Lady Blanche* service between New Providence and Exuma Cays from February 1977 to May 1986: 120,160 miles and 12,016 hours.

• *Lady Blanche* substituted service between New Providence and Central Eleuthera from February 1977 to April 1983: 41,600 miles and 4,160 hours.

• *The Grand Master* service between New Providence and Georgetown, Great Exuma Island from May 1986 to January 2004: 263,220 miles and

26,322 hours.

The grand total of combined mileage and hours on the sea from 1968 to 2004 was 586,210 miles and 58,621 hours. These hours do not include taking on and unloading cargos, three to four days at docks, or hours travelled at night. He was at the helm approximately 75 percent of the time.

He was considered the best captain at night, especially travelling throughout the Exuma Cays during the decades of 1960 and 1970 when aids to navigation were little or none at all on land, sea and ship. Those of you who know the area, could you imagine going through Galliot Cut on a pitch dark night in extremely rough seas and bad weather, with the ship rocking from side to side, up and down, and you cannot see a thing ahead or around you to steer the ship in the right directions? This is just one of my father's many lifetime challenges. But he always had his ancient and modern GPS with him – "God Positioning System."

As Senior Master on both the *Lady Blanche* and *The Grand Master* from 1977 to 2004, my father had not taken a vacation nor time off. He never missed a trip as Master all those many years, and he never stopped working, even to rest. He served his people well, and he served his people faithfully.

My father will go down as the best mail boat captain the Bahamas has ever seen, and the greatest sailor in Bahamian history.

During his sloop racing career from 1954 to

2005, he dominated sloop racing and inspired many sailors, fans and foreigners alike. There was none like him before, and there they may not be another after, to carry on and continue the tradition like my father.

His record and achievements during his more than half a century as a sloop skipper is an outstanding one, matchless in many ways.

During the first Out Island Regatta at Georgetown, Exuma, in 1954, he was the first double regatta champion with his sloop *Marie* in Class A and *Sea Hound* in Class C.

He won the first and only National Family Island Regatta that was held outside of Georgetown in New Providence during the Bahamas Independence Celebration in 1973.

In 1968, during the Bahamas Games and 25th Independence Anniversary celebrations in New Providence, he won both the Gold Medal and Silver Jubilee Celebration races.

He was the first skipper to set a racing record at the National Family Island Regatta that is still standing: five straight wins in the Class A sloop with *Tida Wave*.

He won thirteen National Championship races in Class A on three different sloops: *Marie*, *Lady Muriel* and *Tida Wave*, and seven Prime Minister's Cup Championship races – more than any sailor to date.

He won ten Class C Championship races in the National Family Island Regatta on two boats:

Sea Hound and *Spray Hound*.

He won three straight Marlboro Championship of Sailors Elimination Races in New Providence on *Tida Wave* from 1981 to 1983.

From 1954 to 1999 during the 20th Century, he was the only skipper to have won one or more Class A Championships in every decade.

My father didn't need any polishing. He was polished and shining from his birth to his death, and his polish never came off.

To the best of my knowledge and understanding, and to the best of my ability, many of you can say the same about my father.

He envied no man. He spoke no ill words against any man. He fooled no man. He spoke no false accusation against any man. He took nothing by false acquisition from any man. He boasted to no man. He complained to no man. He worshipped no man. He worshipped no material things. He was fair and honest to all men. He cared for all men. He had a heart of peace and a love for all men. He was kind. He gave much more to his friends than he every received. He always lent a listening ear to all. He was a confidante. He was modest. He was a pillar of strength. He was our earthly guard and protector, a disciplinarian and a true friend.

He was a gentleman of the first order.

He was a national hero of the first order.

He was our national champion of the first order.

He was a real legend.

Most of all, he was a God fearing man.

I can truly say that my father believed that God was always in control and all of his successes would not have been possible without God's grace and guidance.

My father and his family had an excellent relationship. We all trusted him and he loved us all. He trusted us and took care of us. All of his hard work and labour over almost seven decades was done for us all. He never grumbled nor complained about it. We cannot let him down. We have to continue walking the road he walked on. His road had no detour, no turning back, everything straightforward.

He put Staniel Cay on the map for us. He left Staniel Cay on the map for us. It's our duty and responsibility to keep Staniel Cay on the map. We cannot let anyone come and take it from us. We have to let the world know that Staniel Cay is still Gray Cay and we would like to keep it Gray Cay.

The road was long, the race was long. The course was long, the seas were rough. The waves were high, the wind was strong. The tide was strong, the battle was long.

The road had no detour and was rocky at the beginning, becoming smoother toward the end. The armour was heavy, it was a heavy load to bear.

The battlefield is clear now, the battle over. He won his battle.

I would like to express my sincerest thanks to

all the sailors, crew members, family members, friends, associates and fans both inside and outside our beloved country, for your support and cheers and your love for such a great man.

There is nothing to add to this tribute. May Capt. Rolly Gray rest in peace.

Yeocomico

In the early 1980s, Bob Chamberlain and Joe Hocher decided to upgrade the yacht club. The little bar, which could seat about a dozen people, was no longer practical as self-serve.

In the early years of the club, those who poured their own kept track of their tab and generally paid the correct amount, other than a few that maybe slipped by toward the end of an evening.

Old times were passing, however. Although visitors, mostly yachtsmen, thought it was a novel idea, the bar began to lose whatever profit it had made in earlier years, given the amount of liquor and beer consumed compared to what was being put into the cash box. They decided to make it a "real bar."

Bob and Joe also realized the necessity of providing more power to the more sophisticated sail and power boats now visiting the Exumas. It was no longer a sleepy little fuel stop. Now the cottages were booked and people were arriving by air as well as by sea. And, knowing how thirsty everyone gets at the end of a long day in the sun, a fully equipped bar with a paid bartender would quickly turn the deficit into a profit.

A135 KW Caterpillar generator was ordered, and a new bar was designed to accommodate at least 20 stools. Racks to hold all the fancy bar glasses, sinks, coolers, a soda machine and other bar items were added to a growing list of necessities for the big club upgrade.

Since so many other large items were also needed, they ordered lumber to improve and expand the docks, as well as concrete block for all the planned building projects. There were ice machines, storage racks for the walk-in freezers and coolers...the list grew to fill a freight boat. We added a golf cart, as did Harry "O." By the time the *Yeocomico* left Fort Lauderdale, she was loaded down.

Harry decided to ride with the captain to handle the paper work and to see that the cargo arrived safely, as he was familiar with the Exuma waters with its numerous sand spits and variety of islands. This was before GPS, Loran and all the other gadgets that have taken the worry (and guessing) out of navigation.

They crossed the Gulf Stream and were headed toward North Bimini Rock to take the northerly route to Nassau via the Northwest Channel light.

As they headed to North Bimini Rock, Harry made the comment to the captain that they were getting awfully close.

"The captain told me he'd been through here many times and that he could get so close he could piss on it," said Harry. "I shrugged my shoulders and went below for some much needed sleep."

Within minutes, he was thrown forward as the freight boat hit bottom and plowed to a halt, grounding hard on the reef, dead in the water.

"I came back up and there it was, North Bimini Rock, right off the railing," said Harry. "The captain looked a little dumbfounded, then made a comment about all those damn concrete blocks changing his waterline."

A distress radio call was made, and I was notified at the office on our single side-band radio that the boat had gone up on North Bimini Rock with all the cargo.

While I did not maintain a log of all the events that occurred, I did write "The Wreck of the Yeocomico" to the tune of "The Edmund Fitzgerald," which serves as a brief outline of what happened.

Harry knew the first persons to contact were Joe Hocher and Marcus Mitchell, who already had started Overseas Salvage. They never received the first radio call for help, but I was able to relay what had happened from Fort Lauderdale to the yacht club.

Joe loaded his single engine plane with old inner tubes, scuba tanks and pumps. He and Marcus had become experts at keeping boats afloat with their system.

Trey left the island for Bimini with more salvage gear on our plane, plus Marcus and Chris, who had his boat at the yacht club.

When they arrived, *Yeocomico* was bursting with all the dock lumber, the golf carts were going head to head and randomly turning on, rolling back and forth on the deck as the sea rolled the boat, and the 135 KW generator was listing precariously.

Three freight vessels that were in the area came to the rescue: the *Humble*, the *Connie* from Cat Cay and *Island Trader*. None could get close enough to offload cargo.

Then the *Caicos Cloud* arrived, and she was able to transfer the cargo to her decks and holds. The *Connie* then took everything back to Fort Lauderdale to begin the process all over again.

"We worked for three days and nights offloading the cargo," said Harry. "We salvaged almost everything but the concrete block. As we left, the native wrackers came to plunder what was left as *Yeocomico* broke up."

My last verse:

> *The end of this tale is yet to be told,*
> *The cargo in Lauderdale.*
> *And when all the bills were added up,*
> *It could have been sent by mail.*

Money

Without a bank or ATM on the island, it's often been necessary to shuffle funds back and forth to the States or Nassau, with aircraft pilots often serving as couriers, and trust with a capital "T" for all involved.

When we sold one of our airplanes to our Bahamian pilot, we told him he had to give us U.S. dollars, not Bahamian funds. He made the downpayment, then several incremental payments that were always under the legal limit for bringing funds back into the States.

When the final $30,000 was due, he arrived on our cottage doorstep with a grocery bag of smelly bills, none greater than a twenty, but all U.S. currency.

After our first "you've got to be kidding me," he explained that he had traveled all over the Bahamas to friends and relatives, exchanging his Bahamian bills for any U.S. currency that people were hoarding. I think some of it was buried under rocks for how it looked and smelled.

It took the better part of a day to organize and count the money, but he did show up with $30,000 in U.S. cash.

Going through U.S. Customs, we declared the money, but

when it came to counting it, the official held his breath, looked at us in disbelief, and declined tallying it up. We returned later with a copy of the deposit ticket to confirm the amount.

In the course of all the years servicing the island by air, we were asked to take back small increments of funds for people on boats. One such case was a gentleman who needed to get funds to a lawyer to help him in a drug case before turning himself in to authorities. They had money stuffed in cat food boxes, under bunks, in hidden compartments on the boat...we would bring some back time and again and put it in our floor safe at home.

One night, just for grins, we played Monopoly with the real money.

The Millenium "Bug"

Vivian Rolle summarized the year with one statement: "The Millenium Bug did not infect the internet or computers. It bit Staniel Cay."

2000 was a year of tragedy.

These stories are included because they reflect the character and community of Staniel Cay, where all join as one to help when needed.

January 2000

On January 14, 2000, the *Etienne and Cephas*, bound for Nassau from Staniel Cay with 13 crew and passengers, ended almost 14 years of continued freight boat service throughout the islands.

"She had a good run," said Capt. Etienne Maycock, who with his brother, Capt. Cephas, ran the boat for almost fourteen years. "She hit every port and every island in the Bahamas that has mail service, substituting for every mail boat in the Bahamas."

Her main run was to the Ragged Islands, where the Maycocks originate. "After the *Lady Blanche* stopped service to the Exumas, we took over her run."

Before recounting the final hours of his vessel, Capt. Etienne explained that the *Etienne and Cephas*, like many freight boats in the Bahamas, was built in St. Augustine.

"At the time she was built there was a huge demand for freight boats. The wood came from different places and the boats were not as seaworthy as they should have been," he said. "Of all the boats made during that time, only the *Current Pride* is still running. *Lady Blanche, Spanish Rose, Capt. Moxey*, the *Central Andros Express*...all of them are gone."

The *Lady Blanche* was declared unseaworthy and was towed to Arawak Cay, where old abandoned boats go to rest in Nassau.

On that day in January, the *Etienne and Cephas* left the Exumas early morning with good weather and a flat calm sea. The boat arrived at Staniel Cay about mid-day, and when they departed the weather was still good.

"By the time we got to Elbow Cay we saw dark clouds, a cold front approaching," said the captain. "We continued on as there was no place to seek shelter, with everyone still comfortable. It was a summer squall that often produces water spouts, so we were especially alert. As the weather got worse, we filled drums with water to keep the boat down, as she was extremely light after unloading all her freight."

In less than an hour the wind went from zero to 45-50 miles per hour.

"I took the helm from Cephas and did my best to keep the boat on course, feeling we could still make it to port. Then she started 'spanking,' the bow pounding head on into the seas. As she rested in-between the waves you could hear the wood. To be honest, I thought she had sprung a plank, but then she started doing okay and I relaxed. But then for some reason she began tipping.

The engine and generator were still running, but when they checked the engine room, the engines were half covered with water.

"We radioed Highbourne Cay and told them we were taking water. I knew then we would have to abandon ship, so the decision was made to get the life rafts down and ready during daylight in case we had to ride out the night," he said. "All the passengers were told to put on life vests and we strapped the two life boats together."

He explained that the rafts were equipped with eight days of food and water for 25 people.

"Highbourne contacted BASRA (Bahamas Air and Sea Rescue Association)," he said. "We watched as the boat took on water. She never went totally down because of her airtight tanks in the bow and the freezer down below. She eventually headed down with her props out of the water, then she flipped to the side. After it got dark we couldn't see."

He said the wind blew from that Friday until the following Wednesday. When a Coast Guard helicopter could finally fly, they couldn't find the vessel. The following week, when the mailboat came from Andros, they saw debris and pieces of the *Etienne and Cephas*. She had drifted down along the Tongue of the Ocean and broke on a reef.

"It's sad in a way," said Capt. Etienne. "I knew I had to get another freight boat as we had a secure route. Once you have a secure mail boat contract, the banks are willing to help you." He said seventeen mailboats currently cover the island nation.

While Capt. Etienne still hears the call of the sea, his older brother lost his love for the boat. He told Etienne he wanted to stay ashore, but that he'd be there if Etienne ever needed him.

The *M/V Captain C* was built of steel in New Orleans, and Capt. Etienne again runs his route from Nassau to the Exumas and Ragged Island.

***

Burke Smith of Staniel Cay, also recalled that memorable event.

"The sea was smooth when we left Staniel Cay, and we didn't have much freight, just some propane tanks and a few other things going back to Nassau," he said. "The wind picked up when we got north of the Elbows off Little Pigeon Cay (near Shroud Cay) and the sea got rough."

The boat was riding the heavy seas when it smacked down on a wave and he heard a large "pow."

"A plank had cracked open and we started taking water," he said. "The pump was going but the water poured in so fast it shut it down. Then it reached the engine and shut it off. Marvin, one of the crew, told everyone to get their life jackets. In about an hour time, she was nose down. When I came out of my room with my life jacket water was already running toward the stern."

Capt. Etienne Maycock radioed a "May Day" as soon as the plank broke and ordered the life boats be prepared.

"We all got in the two life boats with only our suit on our back," said Burke.

A helicopter came from Nassau, then two other mail boats came. Because there were so many gas tanks in the water, The *Teresa M* was advised to stay away as a BASRA Defense

Force boat was under way from Coral Harbor.

"They picked us up and took us to Nassau," said Burke.

Was he frightened?

"No. It was the fourth time I was shipwrecked," he smiled.

Curious, I asked him to tell me about the others.

"The first time I was in a small conching boat from Black Point, about 22 feet long, with my two brothers, Cecil and Willard," he said. "We were anchored off Fowl Cay, sleeping aboard because the camp on Fowl Cay (near Rocky Dundas islands) wasn't large enough to sleep all of us. The anchor dragged while we were sleeping and we would have been swept out Conch Cut if she hadn't hit the rocks."

There was a hole in the side of the boat where she went up. They crawled out, bundled up, and in daylight were able to nail a piece of canvas over the opening and "take it around to harbor."

The second shipwreck happened sailing from Green Cay to Nassau in a sailboat smack named *The Greyhound*, about 24 feet long.

"We were coming around the eastern point of New Providence," he recalled. "We had to drop down sail to get into Nassau and were blown up on the rocks. We got into a little dinghy and sculled ashore."

The third time was off Little San Salvador, now called Half Moon Cay, between Cat Island and Eleuthera.

"We were fishing on *The Greyhound* and hit a reef that night," he recalled. "The sea was in a rage, beat us over the bow. We didn't sink, but rubbed the keel when a big swell sent us over the reef. She didn't take on any water and we were able to sail into Cat Island that night with half the keel ripped off."

June 2000

Fire has always been a worry on the island. If a hurricane is coming, you can prepare. Fire has a way of instilling immediate fear, and in June 2000, the island rallied for the biggest fire drill ever. A house was burning on South Staniel.

Lynn Green, a homeowner, had just left the yacht club in his golf cart about 10:30 p.m. on a Saturday with his son, teen-age daughter and her school friend. As they approached the airport on their return home, he saw a fire in the distance.

"I drove along the airstrip and was horrified as I realized Runaway, a home near the end of the runway, was on fire," said Lynn. "We raced home as fast as we could to call the yacht club on VHF radio as I didn't have a hand-held with me. It was the longest ride in the world."

Once the word was out, everyone on the island showed up, not only to save the house, but the island. Everything was very dry, and the fire was jumping in all directions. About 50 people answered the call: local residents, guests at the yacht club and people off boats. Ray, the park warden, was also on the island and helped throughout the night.

Vivian Rolle said when residents first reached the fire and saw people already fighting it, they ran home for buckets and shovels.

"At one time, Sandy Malcolm had dug water holes all over South Staniel with the idea of eventually doing a reservoir, which he never did," she said. "We knew where these holes were, and directed where to cut through the brush. There was one behind Rum Punch, and then we found the one behind the old McMillan house, very close to the fire. A human chain formed to dump buckets of water on the fire."

Lynn said there were about seven people in the bucket

brigade, including his son, Lynn, Jr.

"George Robertson, who owned Islandaire next door, got his four-wheeler in action, hauling 5-gallon buckets of sea water from the beach to the fire," he said. "As the fire approached the middle part of the island, Pat Lapide of Goat Point brought his back hoe and started digging trenches. He also cleared brush away from the Robertson house and dug a trench between them as the fire was rapidly burning in that direction."

Vivian said, "Fire carries its own wind," and a team of people had to start dumping water on the abandoned McMillan house as embers had already begun charring the dry structure. The fire was so intense that a propane tank exploded and burst into the air.

The winds were extremely strong, blowing from east to west, with hot air rising as the fire burned.

"All of a sudden you'd see a leaf or a piece of the house rise in the air and travel 50 or 100 yards toward the center of the island where it was extremely dry. We couldn't even see where the fire was spreading. All of us with homes on South Staniel were deathly afraid the fire was going to take the whole end of the island," said Lynn. "People were wild-eyed, yet everyone was on autopilot, relentlessly fighting the fire."

He said they worked all night, through dawn, until about 6:15 a.m.

"I knew my son was in the bucket line, but I didn't know he was first, the one to pour water on the fire," he said. "When it was almost out, someone came to tell me my son was badly hurt. He had lost his balance throwing the last bucket on some embers and had fallen into the fire. His hands and feet had second degree burns. Larry (Romaine), who is half the size of my son, picked him up and carried him 200 yards to safety without skipping a beat, then he was rushed to the clinic. By the time I arrived, nurse Mary Lou Fadden was already debriding his skin from the muscles on his hands, which were three times their normal size. George Robertson urged me to get him off the island. I knew my neighbor, Ron Spivey, was flying out that day. It turns out he slept through the whole incident, and thankfully, was ready to go by 7 a.m. He took me and my son directly to Opa Locka, where an ambulance was waiting to take him to Jackson Memorial in Miami. I stayed with him and everyone on the island took care of my daughter, Kristin, and her friend until we returned several days later."

Even though everyone thought the fire was out, Vivian said after church services on Sunday they could see the fire burning again near the McMillan house.

"The fire had burned under ground and reached a pile of plywood. We fought all afternoon, soaking the ground so that there wasn't a speck of fire left," she said. "This time it was out for good."

Lynn said to this day, when he arrives at the island, the first thing he's asked is how his son is doing.

"I know they held a prayer service for him, and Rhonda always asks, 'How's my boy?' Staniel Cay has such an incredible sense of community, with everyone pulling together. It's a special place."

Runaway was totally rebuilt over a long process and is, once again, enjoyed by its owners.

There is now a portable fire extinguisher at the airstrip, and several home owners have put in personal fire-fighting systems to pump water from the sea.

July 2000

In those days, Vivian and Berkie Rolle were my caretakers for Serenity cottage. Vivian did the cleaning and laundry, and Berkie handled the maintenance. I would give them the schedule, they would meet my people, check them out, and make sure everything was okay.

On July 8, 2000, I was visiting my mother in Wisconsin, getting ready to return to Florida the next day. I had very little cell phone reception, but the phone would tell me I had messages. I realized I was suddenly getting several calls, so drove about five miles for good reception. One of the calls was from my renters from the island, saying because of the accident they didn't know what to do, where to go...

My heart sank. I called the island and couldn't get in touch with anyone, but finally I reached Millicent Kelly, and she told me a little bit of what happened. I called my son, John, in Fort Lauderdale, and asked him to be in touch with the island and to handle anything that needed to be done, that I didn't have any details, but something horrible had happened.

Vivian recalls the day as if it were yesterday.

"I was cleaning Serenity cottage for the next guests. I remember it was the first time I didn't turn on the VHF radio when I arrived. I had decided to just do what I had to do and rush back home because there was a lot to do that day, as Saturday was turnover day for several rentals."

She finished the cottage about 10:30 a.m. and was walking down the hill to the yacht club. She thought it strange that no one was underneath the gazebo.

"Usually, several of the local boys would be there," she said. "As I passed the yacht club, there wasn't a sound, again, very unusual."

When she reached the Hocher house, she met a lady who was going back to the yacht club.

"She said she had heard about an accident, but didn't know who it was," said Viv. "She said they had been calling for doctors on the radio...hadn't I heard them? I told her that I had not been listening to the radio."

Fred (Allen) Rolle was standing in front of his house when she passed by and he asked her if she knew who's plane had crashed at the airport. I had this horrible feeling.

"When?" I asked.

"He told me it was about 10:30. I couldn't hear anything that far away at Serenity. I knew Roland was going out about that time to carry Pam and Glen of Crow's Nest. I hoped..."

She decided to cut back through the village, and when she got to Roland's house, she saw Eloise Smith, who asked Vivian if she knew what had happened.

I said, "I hope it's not Roland."

When she reached Marvin's house, she noticed three Black Point boats at the Isles General dock, and mentally wondered why they were there.

"When I came around the bend, I saw a big crowd at the airport. I asked, 'What happened, what happened?' Jackson Miller was here and was supposed to fly out that morning. He and another person told me not go to the airport. He said Berkie ain't got no hand."

She looked at the crowd at the airport gazebo and remembers asking, "Berkie?" Several people tried to hold her back, telling her not to go there. They knew that Berkie's truck had been hit and almost totally demolished by a landing plane that tried desperately to avoid him as he crossed the runway.

"I said, don't go there? That's my HUSBAND out there."
She broke loose and ran. They already had Berkie in a twin-
engine Aztec that had just dropped off some people.

"I got to the plane and they said I couldn't come. I said,
you're going to tell me I can't come and he's my husband?"

Mary Lou Fadden, Staniel Cay's volunteer nurse of many
years, let her talk to Berkie.

"He was groaning and I could see it was serious. I told
him I'm coming back."

Greg Pruitt, who also had his plane at the airport, and his
wife Pam, told Vivian to go to the house and get all her
papers. She assumed she'd be flying with him to Nassau.

"I went back, grabbed his pouch with passport and insurance papers, and my traveling purse with all my documents,"
she said. "When I got back to the airport, Greg was gone. I
thought I was going to die. Greg went and left me?"

Then someone explained that Greg had taken Gwen Johnson, who had been in the truck with Berkie, to Nassau, with
nurse Beverly from Black Point and Mary Lou's daughter,
also a nurse who had just arrived at the island, to help Gwen,
who had neck and thigh injuries.

"Roland was still there, so I went to Nassau with him,
Pam and Glen. It was the longest flight in history," she said.
"I thought the plane would never reach. It's such a powerless
feeling."

By the time they got to Nassau, the ambulance had
already taken Berkie to Princess Margaret and another ambulance was loading Gwen.

Nurse Mary Lou, who was in ER trauma for years in the
States before coming to the island, said she got a call from
Sharon Smith telling her to go to the airport, that there was an

emergency.

"That's all she would say," said Mary Lou. "My daughter, also a nurse, had just arrived, so we went to the airport figuring it was probably some little old lady getting on or off a plane. We could see Berkie's truck and also a hat on the runway and I thought it was Vivian's hat."

They parked and went to the plane, and realized it was Berkie and Gwen.

"We started to take care of them right away," she said. "I sent someone back to the clinic for the litter. Greg Pruitt, a doctor with a home on the island, came and couldn't believe I was keeping Berkie's blood pressure stable. I wanted Berkie to go right to Ryder in Miami, but the Exuma pilots said they had 'good enough in Nassau.' I believe if he had gone directly to Miami he would still have an arm."

She put the arm together as it was still attached, wrapped it so he wouldn't bleed to death, and packed it with ice. There was no time to start an IV and she didn't have gloves. When they arrived in Nassau, the paramedics didn't want to hear anything from her.

"I told them if they took his shoe off, which they wanted to do, his foot would fall off. They finally listened."

Several family members were already in Nassau by the time Vivian arrived, including her sister, Edith Toote, and Theresa Cooper. Everyone went to the hospital.

The doctor at Princess Margaret had once worked with Greg Pruitt at Jackson Hospital in Miami, so he put Greg in charge of letting the family know what was happening.

"Greg told me that is was very bad, and that they really couldn't do anything in Nassau, but said if we could get him to Jackson Hospital in Miami, they could possibly save his foot." The brake rod had gone through his right foot and was still in place where they had cut it off.

He told her Jackson Memorial needed a deposit of $5000 to take him.

"Here it was, Saturday morning. Greg said we'd have to find people to get money to Jackson, that if we had insurance it could work," she said. "I almost shouted that we had insurance, and produced the insurance card. He called Jackson, gave them the information, and they said they would set up everything, including an air ambulance."

Vivian said that year the insurance premium had gone so high on their major medical that they had considered cancelling, as they hadn't used it for several years.

"We really thought about it, then decided to keep it for another year because we had put so much into it already to have it lapse now. I think God made that decision."

The air ambulance was due at 6 p.m., but because of afternoon thunderstorms between Miami and Nassau, it didn't arrive until about 8 p.m. Vivian and Edith went with Berkie to Miami, where they arrived about 8:45 p.m. Berkie had been given nothing for his pain until he arrived at Ryder Trauma at Jackson Memorial Hospital. It was so intense that he didn't even know what was happening.

"Everything was ready for him when we arrived," said Vivian, "the ambulance, the operating room, a team of doctors. One doctor told me that because of the way his leg and hand were hurt, it would take about 19 hours in the operating room."

Jim Sherman, a Florida resident with a home on South Staniel, had heard about the accident and met Vivian at the hospital. My son, John, and Joe Hocher also made it to the hospital that night. When Jim heard how long the operation would take, he took a room at Day's Inn as he had a long drive back to his home, and paid for an extra three nights for Vivian and Edith.

"When they told me the operation was going to be so long, I pleaded with the doctors to save his hand, telling them that he plays the guitar and organ in church. They did what they could, but told me if they tried to save his hand, they could lose him. By amputating, they could save his life. I told them that if that's the choice, to take it off."

By Monday morning, I was back from Wisconsin and at the hospital. Barry Tendler, who has Swept Away on South Staniel, had flown in the night before from Cape Cod, where they spend the summer, leaving his wife Suzanne to run their motel. Greg Pruitt arrived from the island with "Mother" Jane White, who has always been close to Berkie's family, often preaching as a guest minister in Staniel Cay's baptist church and living at their home.

I can recall walking into Ryder Trauma and joining Vivian, Mother White and Barry in the lounge, waiting for Berkie to wake after the long surgery. Barry kept asking, "Why Berkie? He always looks before crossing the runway."

In fact, he had stopped and looked. He and Gwen both looked to the north and south, but the plane that hit the truck had already descended and was below the top of the hill on the north end of the runway, blending into the terrain. He couldn't hear the plane over the noise of the truck's engine. The pilot saw Berkie stop, and figured he saw him. To his horror, Berkie started driving across as he touched down. He tried to go around, but didn't have enough room on the runway to clear the truck, so the prop actually cut through the steering column and wheel. The pilot knew Berkie and felt terrible, but there was nothing he could have done. Fortunately, the pilot and his passenger received only minor injuries and the plane was able to leave the airstrip after some minor maintenance and installation of a new propeller.

That night at home, I fell asleep worrying about Berkie, thinking of how bad he must be hurting after seeing him that day, and Barry's question. About 3 o'clock in the morning I awoke with a start. It was as if someone hit me over the head, and I clearly heard a deep voice say, "Because I have other plans for him." I could hardly sleep the rest of the night.

The next day I told Vivian and Mother White about the dream. Vivian just smiled, and said Berkie had been contemplating the ministry.

Before telling me the rest of the story, it's also timely to tell of a dream Vivian recalled while at Day's Inn about two weeks after the accident.

"This is the strangest thing, but I can recall it vividly," she said. "I had the dream about three months before. There was some kind of an accident in the dream, but all I knew was that Berkie was hurt. I saw a team of doctors and nurses, all dressed in white, but the nurses had green gowns over their white uniforms as if ready for surgery. They came pushing Berkie down this long hallway. One nurse told me they were rushing him to the operating room. I kept asking them what happened but they never told me. They rushed him through this big iron door with a round porthole. No one paid any attention to me except for the one nurse. I saw Berkie on the gurney, strapped down from head to foot and covered like a mummy, but his left arm was hanging over the trolley. I went to the door, looked through the window, and asked the Lord to not let him die, to please save his life. I know that God often allows dreams to happen to strengthen you. All I can think about now was his hand hanging off that gurney in the dream. I never thought to ask God to save his hand, only his life. I often wonder if it would have made a difference, but I know the dream was preparing me to make the decision to save his life."

She accepts the fact that it was just too long a time between the accident at 10:30 a.m. to 11 p.m. when they started surgery, to save his hand, and the doctors had to do so much more to save his life. He had five broken ribs, three broken toes on his right foot, his shoulder was damaged and his left leg was bare to the bone from the steering column slicing off all the flesh.

"The doctor told me to be prepared, that he might not walk for two years."

At first, Vivian spent as much time as possible in the hospital, but after a couple of days, a nurse pointed out that the chair in Berkie's room was actually a bed. From that point on, she was by his side 24/7, making sure he was comfortable, giving him water, reading the Bible.

"The doctors and nurses at Ryder Trauma did an excellent job," she said, "but patients need family by their side for the little things."

Berkie had so many visitors from all over the Bahamas, the United States and other countries, that those at the front desk at Ryder wanted to know who he was. A dignitary? The prime minister? They had never seen so many visitors for any patient, black or white.

During that time, a special visitor came to witness, telling Berkie that he was called to the Ministry, that the enemy had tried to destroy him and that God himself had saved him from death.

Berkie gained strength, God lifted his pain, and he defied all predictions. The doctors could only attribute his remarkable progress to his strong faith. He stayed in Ryder Trama Center until October, then joined Vivian and Mother White at Day's Inn, where they stayed until January.

The day after Thanksgiving, I had invited Berkie and Vivian for dinner. I emptied my trunk so there would be room for a wheelchair, and drove to Miami. I was stunned. Berkie slowly came out of the motel room using a walker. It was like witnessing a miracle.

In January, they moved to Barry's Miami condominium with a beautiful view of Biscayne Bay. Vivian flew back to the island once or twice a month to tend to business, but while she was in Miami, her sister Millicent, niece Samantha, Terri MacGregor and Sue Johnson of South Staniel, kept everything going on the island, including the store and caretaking of various rental homes.

Vivian returned to Staniel Cay in April 2001 to clean and prepare the house, and Berkie and Vivian returned to the island for a homecoming in May, 2001. They continued to travel to Miami for the next two years for checkups, but he was soon back working at the Staniel Cay Yacht Club and their Isles General store.

He wears a prosthetic arm and hand for when he wears a suit, mostly in church, but he has adapted to using one arm. Although he can no longer play the guitar, he has mastered the organ using one hand and his feet. Berkie is truly a walking miracle, and inspiration to everyone now as pastor of Mount Olivette Baptist Church.

Vivian said Berkie's story was in many of the Ryder Trauma newsletters, and will be included in a book on its outstanding patients.

September 2000

This was the month the telephone tower collapsed, killing two workers who had come from Nassau to replace some of the rusting cross pieces. They were about half way up when the tower buckled, landing within a couple of feet of the school where the children were in session. It just missed the telephone building, open for business.

Penny Nixon, who was working in the Batelco office at the time, said it was a routine day. Three workers, who had been working on the tower several times before, had started at the top of the tower and were working their way down, replacing parts that had rusted.

"They had already worked all morning," she said. "Close to noon, there was a loud screeching sound, like the building was being torn down. I jumped up, went outside, and saw the tower on the ground, wrapped around the building. I saw the workers, who were friends of everyone on the island. Two of them were killed instantly."

Tourists and villagers rushed to the scene. The children, just let out of school for lunch break, were kept away from the disaster.

"I ran inside to get some communication," she said, "but the VHF was gone. Everyone was trying to find a radio to reach Highbourne Cay to let them know communications were down. A big boat was finally able to get through."

It was four months before a new, larger tower would be completed.

November 2000

While telephones were being routed through various other towers so there would be some communication on the island, Staniel Cay had another tragedy. One moonless night, *The Grand Master* freight boat, bound for Georgetown from Nassau, was approaching Harvey Cay light on its way to Dotham Cut and Exuma Sound when it hit an old vessel with no lights loaded with illegal Haitians. There was no warning, no way of knowing they were off Harvey Cay with countless people on board. Many drowned, but about 80 were taken aboard *The Grand Master* and other boats alerted of the accident by VHF radio. The survivors were brought to the church at Staniel Cay, where they were tended to and fed by many local residents. They were taken to Nassau, and it is believed they were eventually sent back to Haiti.

Building The New Serenity

For several years, every time I visited my little Serenity cottage, I would doodle designs for a larger structure. While perfect for a vacation getaway, the cottage and bunkhouse were not suitable as a permanent home for retirement. With less than 6,000 square feet all downhill on rock, it was a huge challenge. A conventional home limited the usable square footage because it took up so much of the lot. Plus, I wanted a separate cottage for family and guests.

I had admired the round design of a home on South Staniel, erected in the early 1970s. The company that produced the home was the forerunner of Deltec Homes out of North Carolina, noted for their round design and features for hurricane protection. When Barry and Suzanne Tendler built Swept Away, the first Deltec on Staniel Cay, I fell in love with the design, the use of space, the beautiful panoramic views and, most of all, the construction.

I had gone through the building process and also the renovation process of two previous homes, and in my public relations, graphics and advertising business, had worked closely with architects, builders and developers for many years, producing brochures and marketing plans for projects from ground breaking to sellout. I had observed and understood the construction process and felt confident the Deltecs would be the easiest possible build on the island, given the many drawbacks inherent in an out-of-the-way place with such a small population.

For two years, I played around with Deltec's design templates on my computer, trying to figure the best possible combination for my small lot that would give me everything I wanted in a home and guest cottage at a price I could afford. I finally settled on a 10-side design for the cottage, and two-story 13-side plan for the house. Deltec approved my floor plans, and the project was finally under way.

It meant selling my Fort Lauderdale home, but after 26 years and both kids raised, I was ready for the change. The real estate market had remained strong for waterfront homes in Fort Lauderdale, so I knew the sale would easily finance my island project. As I worked with Deltec finalizing the plans, I put my home on the market, assuming it would sell quickly. The next month, real estate values began to slide, and I watched the appraised value drop by a few hundred thousand dollars. I was already committed to the construction of my Deltecs, so in desperation, I accepted an offer that was way below my expectations, praying that God would help make it all work. In retrospect, I realize how gutsy I was to proceed with the island project, and once it began, how naive I was on the process. For instance, I thought I could continue running my business in Fort Lauderdale to offset the financial loss in selling my house, but it quickly became apparent that I had to physically be on the island. Some clients understood and stayed with me, but it was a challenge to be creative for them while concentrating on Serenity. There were too many questions to be answered on the spot, and I don't think any of the workers or subcontractors totally understood my vision. The plans were there, but translating to the finished design needed my direction.

First of all, imagine building a home on a small island in the middle of a foreign country where there is no ATM, no Home Depot, no Lowes, where groceries are the size of garages. Add to that the fact that I'm an American woman drawing on resources of a foreign native population.

I decided it would be best to ship everything for both the home and cottage at one time: the floor, roof and wall systems produced by Deltec, all the tile, bamboo flooring, cabinetry, furnishings, plumbing fixtures, air conditioners, appliances – as well as a used construction forklift for demolition of the old cottage and to lift the wall panels in place on the new structures. This was one of the first pieces of heavy equipment brought in by an individual.

Before I had it shipped to the island, I learned how to run it, as I believe if you're going to own something, you should know how it works. By the time Serenity was completed, many new homes and projects were underway, and heavy equipment was common on the island: cement trucks, bulldozers, forklifts, dredging equipment, backhoes...whatever was needed would arrive by barge and be sent back to wherever when its job was done, but in 2004, my forklift was an anomaly.

I won't go into the frustration of waiting for the building permit to be issued with my five containers sitting on the island, because it would only raise my blood pressure, but I will admit I began questioning my sanity in undertaking such a monstrous project. At one point, the blueprints were sent back from Georgetown because they lacked plumbing and electrical schematics. They weren't included in the Deltec plans, and I assumed the plumber and electrician would work with me as the buildings were constructed. I knew what I wanted and how both systems would unfold. I tried to get someone to draw up the simple schematics, but it became a huge problem as no one wanted to take on the responsibility. I finally did both schematics myself with all the proper symbols and the plans were approved.

I couldn't hire Americans, so was limited to local workers, who expected to be paid in cash each week. My kids would go to the bank, withdraw cash, and get it to pilots flying to the island from Fort Lauderdale, who would hand over the cushy envelope each week with a knowing smile.

It was impossible to budget, because at that time there were so many unknowns: price of labor which seemed to fluctuate on a regular basis, building materials that had to be purchased in Nassau, subcontractors that had to be brought in from Nassau because of the island's limited resources and skills, tools that had to be purchased because workers didn't have their own...the list goes on and on.

Nassau is 80 miles away, with the freight boat usually arriving once a week. Lumber and other supplies (from small nails and saw blades to large deck beams and everything in-between) had to be ordered and paid for on Monday for the freight boat to deliver on Wednesday (maybe) from Nassau.

Before Tyrone Cooper, a local contractor, could put in the concrete pilings for the new structures, we had to demolish the original cottage. Tyrone used the forklift to start the knockdown on July 15, 2004, and two days later, it was at the dump. I remember looking at the small heap and realizing how little it was reduced to in the end. While I was excited about the new house and cottage to come, I have to admit the demolition was emotional, as so many good memories took place in that little cottage.

By July 20, Tyrone had laid out where the pilings would go, and workers started jackhammering to put them as deep as possible, to "real Staniel" as the bedrock is called. Some holes went down a couple of feet, others less than that, depending on the rock. All the reinforcing rod was epoxy coated, and the concrete for the pilings was imported from the U.S. to ensure no salt contamination. The water to mix the concrete came from the cistern, which was full of rainwater and preserved in the demolition. It is still in use today as a backup water system, replenished with rain collected on the cottage roof.

Since I no longer had the cottage, my son brought his 43-foot Hatteras to the island for me to live on, which was convenient, comfortable, and much appreciated.

With the cottage demolished, pilings were put in for new construction.

By the end of August, the electric meter had been moved to a pole, all the pilings and floor tie beams were in place for both the cottage and house, and the Deltec materials were organized and staged in the large area where the three roads meet at the bottom of what has become known to my grandkids as "huff and puff hill."

Cottage floor system.

At that point, an independent Deltec advisor arrived to direct the construction of the floor, walls and roof of the cottage, the first structure built. He commented on the good job Tyrone had done with the pilings for both structures, the most important part of the project.

Once the advisor staged the materials at the containers to come to the site, it was like watching a giant jig saw puzzle being put together. Every piece of the house fit perfectly, with all the fasteners, glue and materials needed to put it together. In less than a day the floor system was in, and the next day, the forklift began carrying the wall panels to the site. These were eight foot sections completely finished on the outside

The 8-foot panels, with windows and finished siding already installed, went up in a matter of hours.

with insulation, siding and windows installed. We soon realized the power lines across the road up the hill were too low, and they had to improvise to carry the panels on the forks, rather than in the air with a harness.

When the last cottage panel arrived onsite and they were ready to put up the walls, I found out how strong Deltec builds houses. The construction forklift suddenly lost oil pres-

The last cottage panel is installed after being 'run over' by the forklift.

sure while running, perched on the old concrete steps to the original cottage. Twenty thousand pounds started rolling down the short incline, headed for the cottage that only had the floor installed. At the dock below was the Hatteras. As the huge yellow behemoth started to roll everyone scrambled to get out of the way. We watched in horror as it rolled over the last wall panel, one huge tire going through the window. It stopped when it reached the cottage tie beam, only damaging a small corner of plywood floor. With the heavy forklift sitting on the panel, I thought for sure the project would have to be put on hold waiting for a new one. They got the forklift in gear, backed it up, and other than the broken window, the panel was intact. If you look closely at the wall for the second bedroom, you can still see tire marks. By the end of the second day, the walls were in place, the roof system was almost completed, and some of the workers had started on the floor system for the house. As the last roof truss was placed, Tyrone climbed to the top, raised a white flag and announced, "Serenity is back!"

At that point, there was some talk of a hurricane forming

Tyrone Cooper raises the 'topping off' flag...Serenity is 'back!'

in the lower Caribbean, and it was soon named Frances. Everyone put in long hours in preparation for it possibly hitting the Exumas. More workers were added, and there was a steady sound of air hammers nailing radiant barrier for roof insulation, hurricane strapping from the cottage roof to the piling tie beam, plywood to the cottage roof and the house floor beam system to secure the first floor walls.

As hurricane warnings were posted, everyone also had to prepare their own homes and make plans to possibly leave the island. We secured all the construction materials as best we could, and added more layers of tarp over many of the interior items that were now out of the containers and along the road: cabinets, drywall, lumber, tile, bamboo flooring...it was a lot of stuff!

As the Cooper family boarded up and headed for Nassau, it was decided our Deltec rep would continue to stay in their house, so we made sure he had enough food and water. We got my small boats either out of the water, or moved back to the creek. We unscrewed several dock planks and moved them to high ground so the water would have a place to go and the

Leaving Serenity before Hurricane Frances.

dock could "breathe."

The storm was advancing fast, so we moved the Hatteras to Sampson Cay for safe harborage, towing a Boston Whaler so we could get back and forth before the storm was upon us. I had a sick feeling when we left Serenity the last time before the storm. The cottage had floors, walls and the roof, but was not closed in with soffit and doors. The first floor wall panels of the house were held together by the second floor truss system. The Detecs would soon be tested.

We joined about a dozen boats in the back Sampson Cay marina, which now looked like a spiderweb with extra lines securing all the vessels. We took one of the villas rather than stay aboard, but if I were stranded again in the same situation, I would stay on the boat. It was definitely secure in the marina.

Everyone watched as planks popped off the outside docks

Hurricane Frances pounds Sampson Cay.

and water rose around some of the structures at Sampson Cay. We pooled our resources for food and drinks, and the club gave us use of the kitchen. After we watched the wind literally pick up the island cat and hurl her about 12 feet, we gave her shelter in the villa.

The wind howled constantly as the storm made its way up the Exumas, and I prayed that all was well with Serenity. There was nothing I could do but wait out the storm and hope for the best.

The sea was still very choppy after the storm passed, and it took some time to get back to Staniel in the small boat, but I was thrilled to see everything still standing. The boathouse had some damage, as usual with such storms, but the dock was still standing and the Deltecs looked great from the water. The foliage, a lush green before the storm, was already brown from the salt spray and battering from the wind.

We had a couple more hurricane visits from Jeanne as it wandered around shortly after Frances, but the most we had was lots of rain.

Life returned to normal on the island, and the workers proceeded to finish the second story of the house, now called Retreat, and to get the roof on. Once that was accomplished,

The forklift worked great to install the upper panels on Retreat.

we began moving the tarped goods along the road to the inside of the house. It was then we discovered water and some termite damage (they work FAST!) on some of the kitchen cabinets, drywall and lumber. Some of the hardwood bamboo had mildew, but the termites could only chew the cardboard packaging, not the bamboo itself.

I called my insurance agent, and the adjuster was amazed at how the Deltecs stood up under the storms. She wrote in her report: "I was very impressed with the flooring/roofing system. It looks like that can take a Cat 5! This building is as 'tight as a tick.' The engineering seems to have been done by someone who had their house 'blown away' before. Really, really impressive!"

I was more convinced than ever that I had made the right choice for my island home and cottage. It was back to the business of building. While a couple of workers continued finishing the cottage, most began working on getting the wall panels up on the main house. The construction forklift was

Roof trusses top off Retreat.

able to extend the panels to the second floor, where they were put into place. Within days the roof was on, the whole thing fitting together perfectly. Once both structures were up with the floor, wall and roof systems, it was time for the fun stuff, finishing the inside.

The cottage went fairly fast, but trying to get subcontractors who were busy with other projects was a challenge. The drywall finisher came at night after working all day on another island. When it came time for the tile, someone in the village let the workers delay his job so mine could be done. The local crew from Black Point did a beautiful job tiling the entire bathroom, the floors and also the tumbled marble countertops in the kitchen. As soon as they were done, we were ready for the remaining wood trim and paint.

While various crews worked inside the cottage, another crew worked on the outside deck, which had to cover what was left of the original Serenity cottage, tiled areas where the old kitchen and bath were, the stone patio and also the cistern. By early December the cottage was totally completed with the exception of the bottle gas line for the kitchen stove. I could not get the contractor to hook it up as he was busy with a personal project and I think he knew his job was over at Serenity. As a result, I had to find other accommodations for my first guests over Christmas and New Year's weeks, a disappointment to me as well as them.

After the holidays were over, I reassessed the construction situation and decided to totally give up my business in Fort Lauderdale and take over as full-time general contractor. The main carpenter and his crew agreed to work for me, and we started finishing the house.

When I designed the two structures, I knew I wanted them

to tie together with decking, but didn't know how it would turn out because of the slope of the land to the water. Originally, I had planned for stairs on the outside to go to the top deck of the house, but I decided to eliminate an outside entrance upstairs and only have one entry on the main level for both privacy and security. I remembered some of the stories regarding the original Serenity cottage and how people loved my deck and bunkhouse. No matter how many locks I put on the sliding doors, people somehow managed to get in, but of course, no one would own up to enjoying the place while I was stateside. One native man, after a few beers, told me that Serenity was a favorite place to...he wiggled his hips as if he were doing the twist...that gesture explained it all, and confirmed my suspicions. I did NOT want any "twisting" on my new deck!

Another change to the original plans was to cantilever the deck all the way around the second story after eliminating the stairs. It's perfect for cleaning the windows and for grandkids to expend energy literally running around Grammy's house.

When we began on the first floor of Retreat, I realized I had alloted more space than was necessary for the laundry and downstairs bath area, so I rearranged walls, reduced the size of the laundry area to only what was needed, ordered another toilet and pedestal sink, and ended up with two full bathrooms instead of one. The original plan was for a spacious bathroom with the jacuzzi tub through a sliding door so that only I could have access to the tub. Now I have a full bathroom with the tub and a separate tiled shower.

There were many lively discussions in the course of building. One that almost turned into a shouting match involved the layout of the upstairs. The cottage, with its even 10 sides, made it easy to figure inside walls. With Retreat having 13 sides, there was no way to go corner to corner from one side to the other. I had repeatedly told them to start from dead center of the floor and work out, not from the walls to the center. After three times laying out the walls and seeing a small wedge for the bedroom, I sent everyone home early and told them it would be ready for them in the morning. I got out my square and tape measure, and laid out the floor plan as specified on the blueprints. I tacked down two-by-fours to show where the walls should be, and by morning I was ready for them. They were truly amazed that I was able to measure and cut wood to the specifications.

One disagreement came when I asked them to take down the molding on the eight-foot walls that didn't go to the ceiling. They had put the molding flat side down, as if doing baseboard, instead of inverting it so it tapered to the wall. After arguing unsuccessfully, I finally asked, "Who's paying you?" They looked at me like I was from another planet. "If you want your pay, you'll do it the way I want it."

I then had a discussion about how people were no longer building little plywood cottages on the island, that people planning new houses would expect good workmanship, and that Serenity should be considered a learning experience for jobs to come. I also told them I probably had more patience and understanding of their situation than the new wave of homeowners coming to the island, so it was important we all work together.

Other lively discussions had nothing to do with building. I remember one of the workers commenting that the reason white people want a tan is because deep down they really want to be black. Politics was always a hot topic, and at one point, I threatened to send a worker home if he kept on praising an American in office that I did NOT like. We always ended up laughing, but the guys were very passionate, and loud, with their opinions on just about every topic imaginable. What was significant to me is that they felt comfortable saying anything in my presence, including their feelings on race and some other controversial subjects. There was a lot of teasing and good comradery, and I never had to reprimand a worker for "slacking," as they chided each other to keep up. They arrived at 7:30 every morning, worked until noon, came back at 1 p.m. and worked until 4 p.m. Some days they would stay later if something needed to be finished right away. On the whole, their work ethics were sound.

I think what aggravated the workers the most was all my stuff, which had to be moved from upstairs to downstairs and from one room to another as the house was completed. I didn't like the situation either. I had originally built a 20-by-30 foot structure on a lot I owned on the south side of the island to store all my furnishings and extra building materials, but with costs escalating at Serenity, I decided to sell it, and immediately had a buyer. Everything had to be moved to Serenity, then shuffled around as rooms and floors were completed.

When it came time to arranging furniture, we couldn't find all the special hardware for assembling the dining room table. I came upstairs to find, to my horror, that they were glueing it together with 3M® 5200, a super strength boat caulking compound! The gooey, sticky stuff was everywhere, and I knew it would never hold the legs straight and support the heavy glass top. I also knew it would take 24 hours to cure, and that I would be the one watching that it didn't collapse. What to do? I got some stainless steel three-inch deck screws, showed them where to place them so it didn't look too obvious, and that's what holds it together to this day. Soon after I found the hardware, but by then the 5200 was an integral part of the table.

Another situation arose when I realized they had put the bathroom walls up before putting my L-shaped sofa into the downstairs bedroom. Adding the second full bathroom meant the sofa sections had to go in before the walls were completed. The result is that I have only one side of the couch in that room, which actually worked out better in the end.

Coordinating subcontractors who had to come from Nassau without holding up construction was a challenge, as the plumber, tile man, dry waller, and air conditioner installer were off-island. Thankfully, Stephen Miller, the electrician, lives on the island and was available when needed.

Making sure the right lumber arrived each week was also a challenge, as everything needed to be planned in advance. One of the problems was obtaining pressure treated two-by-twos for all the railings, so we ripped two-by-fours and made our own. I did much of the staining until my back went out and the guys told me to "sit!"

In the States, workers arrive with their own tools, but this was not the case on the island. I had to supply hammers, nail guns, compressor, table saw, drills and bits...everything that was needed for the job. By the end of the project, the guys were referring to my storage room under the house as Home Depot.

The upstairs of the house was livable by May 2005, less than a year after demolition of the original cottage. In July, the grandkids were bathing in the jacuzzi tub in the master bathroom, even though there were no finished walls, only studs awaiting the cement board and tile. The bathroom was not officially completed until April 2006.

With the house finished on the inside by May, we began to work on the landscaping, decking, steps to the dock and many other little touches.

One of the most outstanding additions is my fabulous "bonus room," or "basement." Because the house ended up

Retreat living room with panoramic views.

much higher on the pilings than anticipated due to the sloping terrain, there was substantial headroom under about half of the house toward the water. I had the workers jackhammer and excavate further to give me a sizable storage room, about 300 square feet, under the house. The door opens onto what became the outdoor shower deck which leads to the dock. I'm able to keep freezers, an extra refrigerator, golf cart tires and parts, paint, tools, etc. We saved the soil that was dug out (a precious commodity on this sandy/rocky island) to use for landscaping.

One of the problems has always been getting down to the

dock. The old "Bahama" steps that were cut into the rocky hillside were extremely hazardous. I actually think those steps over the years contributed to me having to have both knees replaced. Marvin Cooper, who fixed a lot of the construction problems toward the end of the project, created a wonderful stairway to the dock, which is now lighted and landscaped.

I had Larry and Elvis build beautiful native rock walls, terracing up from below the decks, and ordered many flow-

Steps to the dock, landscaping walls and coconut tree.

ering plants and trees from Nassau. It's amazing how plants arrive "gift wrapped" on the freight boat. Each plant is wrapped in brown paper, then boxed so it is totally protected. My big palm tree, however, required Larry to jackhammer a three-by-three foot hole in the rock in order to plant it. Top-soil, mulch and peat moss also had to come on the freight boat. Christine in the village gave me a coconut palm she had started, so within a few months, the landscaping toward the water was beautiful. Bougainvillaea, hibiscus, oleander, some lily varieties, seagrapes, desert rose, wedelia and a few other

The old cistern sports a bronze sun sculpture.

varieties added to the tropical setting. It's difficult to keep up, but well worth the effort. I try to use cistern rainwater, because our reverse osmosis city water requires a great deal of fertilizer to help things grow.

I gradually added decorative touches; a bronze sun sculpture on the front of my cistern, a mermaid figurehead where the deck points like the bow of a ship, colorful gheckos, turtles and crabs on the outside storage room wall.

Because I wanted to keep an island feel to the colorful structures, I chose a thatch roof for my golf cart carport. This area also worked great for tables of food and a bar for my house blessing party on April 1, 2007, signifying the official completion of the project. Rev. Berkie Rolle did the honors and everyone on the island was invited.

Both structures are holding up well against the elements, and I'm still happy with all my decisions. Retreat is my primary home. I wake up looking at the incredibly clear turquoise water and go to bed seeing the masthead lights of boats anchored behind Big Major island. I welcome my cottage guests and love my new job as super concierge. Everyone loves the feel and design of Serenity with its comfortable decks overlooking the water. And no one, not even general contractors who have seen the cottage, has guessed that it's less than 700 square feet. Cut off the corners and you gain space. Round is definitely the way to go, especially in these hurricane-prone islands.

Serenity from the air in 2009.

Life in Paradise

Living on an island may sound idyllic, with visions of lying in a hammock, sipping a rum punch, reading a good book and watching the world go by.

In reality, it's a whole different mind set from living in the States. The power might go out for hours at any time of the day or night. For me, this means resetting all the air conditioners when it comes back on. The water may shut off unexpectedly, with a wait for days until a pipe can be fixed. That's why most residents still collect rain water in cisterns, which also means maintaining a pump and pressure tank.

Forget about craving favorite foods. It either comes on the freight boat or you have them flown in at a cost. I've learned to ignore price and be grateful for any goodies that arrive.

Expecting something on the mailboat? It may "reach" or not, depending on that week's "schedule." Even if on time, the boat may have engine or crane problems which can delay delivery for weeks, although this is becoming rare with Staniel Cay's high demand for goods. Other boats usually cover if there is a serious problem with the *Captain C*.

I'll never forget the first time I walked into Isles General and there were fresh sliced mushrooms. I thawed a steak that night and indulged. I also remember the first time fresh broccoli and little yogurts arrived. Living in the States, or just about anywhere else on the planet, you take things like frozen orange juice and milk for granted.

On the flip side, when I return to the States, I usually wait a few days to go into a super market. I can't handle all the choices and shoppers. I've already had to leave all my items in the cart because of my frustration in trying to find something simple. The whole process can be overwhelming when you're used to going in a little store and buying what came in for the week. I can't say I really miss anything, and no one has ever starved on the island.

In the three little grocery stores, however, you'll find the best cheeses, sweet butter from Ireland, home baked bread and even ice cream. Instead of being overwhelmed with thousands of brands of the same item, the choice is always simple and the service splendid.

I will admit, however, that sometimes enough isn't enough. I returned to the island one day to find that my daughter had ordered three dozen Dunkin Donuts which she had flown in on Flamingo Air from Nassau just "because."

Part 3
Island Trivia

This and That

Visitors to Staniel Cay usually have a number of questions after walking, biking, or driving the island. Where does the electric come from? What is the strange fruit on that tree? What are those old structures?

This is a fun chapter that will send visitors on an island treasure hunt. Where to begin?

Most visitors arrive at the airport, where they are greeted with an official welcome-to-the-Bahamas sign.

Visitors are greeted at the airport with this welcome sign.

Airport 'Terminal'

Staniel Cay has an interesting roofed open-air pavilion for people to wait for arriving planes (some visitors have been known to fall asleep on the hard wood benches while waiting for unpredictable arrivals!) that also serves as a notice board for island events. It was a welcome structure in the early 1990s after years of people having to wait in the hot sun. There is also a public phone that has been known to work.

Staniel Cay's open air terminal is a favorite gathering place as people wait for planes.

The only problem is the open-air bush rest room, hopefully solved with the opening of the new yellow customs building when Staniel Cay becomes an official port of entry. I have a standard question when someone says something is going to happen on the island. I ask, "In my lifetime?"

Since it's illegal to land or take off at night except at the few major airports in the Bahamas with control towers, the government installed solar power runway lights on most airstrips in 2009, to be turned on only in emergency by the local police. This is a great relief for residents and visitors, as there have been several medical emergencies that have required evacuation to Nassau or the U.S.

Signs

There are colorful, hand-painted signs throughout the island. This one tells you exactly where to find them.

This sign is located on South Staniel.

Water

In the early 1900s, Staniel Cay had several shallow fresh water wells, but over the years, with the arrival of tourists and the increased demand, they became slightly brackish. Two wells are still in the village, and there are a couple in the over-grown bush. Fresh water has always been a concern. At one time, everyone on the island had a cistern which would hold rain water collected off their roof, but with little rainfall, they often went dry. Because beach sand was used to build the early cisterns, many eventually began to leak as the reinforc-ing rod corroded, breaking or cracking the concrete.

In the 1960s and 1970s, the yacht club and some home

*This 'swimming pool' cistern is behind what was the original
Chamberlain house, next to the cemetery and playground.*

owners had the great idea to enclose the newly manufactured
aluminum above-ground swimming pools to increase their
fresh water holding capacity, covering them with black plastic tarps to keep sunlight from producing algae. One still
stands on the site of the demolished Chamberlain home next
to the cemetery.

Joe Hocher, founder of Watermakers, Inc. and a pioneer
in reverse osmosis (RO), the conversion of sea water to fresh,
began producing fresh water for the yacht club in the mid

This well is still in limited use in the village.

Joe Hocher working in the yacht club shop.

1970s. Now a major world-wide producer of fresh water for islands and yachts, the company was contracted by the Bahamian government in 2003 to produce RO water for the entire island. Initially, sea water was converted, but in 2008, a deep well was tapped for brackish water, making the process more efficient.

Residents with cisterns still collect rain water and those with large capacity still use them as their primary source of fresh water, while those with smaller cisterns use them as

Staniel Cay's fresh water supply is in tanks in back of the school.

backup when a pipe breaks or there is maintenance on the village system.

Electricity

Until 1998, when government power came to Staniel Cay, villagers ran their own generator sparingly if they had one, and relied primarily on kerosene for lights, refrigerator and stove. Propane arrived on the island in the 1980s, so stoves and refrigerators switched to gas. The yacht club and Happy People had their own generators, and vacation home owners often ran generators at considerable cost when in residence. South Staniel residents once had a co-op generator, but it was very small, and residents often accused each other of using too much electricity for such things as toasters and hair dryers.

The government put the main power plant at Black Point, where there is a larger community, and ran underwater cable to Staniel Cay. As more homes were built and air conditioning was no longer a luxury, usage increased at both islands, and backup generators were installed on Staniel Cay. There are occasional short outages, and sometimes voltage is lower than appliances and clocks would prefer, but it sure beats the old days. Eventually, the island may have its own power plant.

Low tide reveals power cables connecting Staniel Cay to Black Point.

Telephones

The island had "real" phone service installed in 1988. Before that, an operator would place a ship-to-shore call via radio through Nassau. The operator would attempt to make the call, but sometimes it was a couple of days before it would go through. The original telephone office is now the local government office. There are commercial

The new telephone tower erected in 2000 after old one collapsed.

phone booths on the island, including one at the Staniel Cay Yacht Club and another at Happy People in the village. There is also a public telephone at the airport.

Flying to the island, I remember the shock of seeing a 200-foot tower where everything had once been flat. The tower marked the first major structural progress on Staniel Cay after the airstrip was constructed in the early 1970s.

Phone booth in front of Happy People and the library.

Clinic

The clinic is located just off the public beach and is staffed by a qualified government nurse, and a doctor comes once a month from Nassau. The nurse handles minor injuries

The clinic is staffed by a government nurse.

and ailments in the clinic, and can help coordinate medical evac to Nassau if there is a more major incident. It's a comfort to know she is there.

Cemetery

Staniel Cay's cemetery is a focal point of the community. If a native dies on the island, the body is sent to Nassau for preparation, and returns within a couple of weeks for service and burial, which is a major event. Family and friends arrive from all points, and the village women prepare food and their homes to accommodate all the visitors, while the men prepare the grave site. Flowers and remembrances adorn

Procession to the cemetery for Emiel 'Tita' Miller in 2006.

the grave for several months, sometimes years.

There is usually a wake the night before, then a "homegoing" service the following day. The procession from the church to the cemetery is a solemn event, with singing and prayers. Following the service, family and friends usually gather in the village for a feast prepared by the women.

Rolly Gray's crypt at the cemetery.

Breadfruit Tree

Staniel Cay is blessed with one breadfruit tree, located next to Happy People in the village. The fruit is very similar to a white potato, and in the old days, Theaziel Rolle (Berkie Rolle's sister who married Kenneth) would slice the fruit very thin and deep fry it, serving the french fry like chips with her famous "Theaziel Burger" at Happy People.

While the tree is native to the South Pacific, where a single tree may produce 200 fruits, those in the Caribbean yield only about 25 per tree, which is about what our Staniel Cay tree produces each year. Breadfruit can be roasted, baked, fried or boiled just like a potato, and is considered a staple food.

There are reports that Lieutenant William Bligh of the HMS Bounty collected and distributed breadfruit as a cheap, high energy food source for British slaves in the Caribbean.

When breadfruit is overripe, the local Bahamians have

Breafruit tree in the village.

used it to make cake and pancakes, and according to Vivian Rolle, the leaves can be boiled as tea to control high blood pressure or to alleviate headache. In days past, the "family people" would strap the big leaves to their heads to protect them from the sun.

There are other plants on the island that can be used for medicinal purposes. Orange berries from the lignum vitae, the heritage tree of the Bahamas, can be eaten to control high blood pressure. Catnip, boiled as a tea, was once used for head cold, belly ache, and whooping cough, or as a poultice for cuts and scrapes on children.

Staniel Cay Artists

Staniel Cay boasts several accomplished artists, and their work is readily available for visitors wanting to take a piece of the island back home with them.

Bernadette Chamberlain, who created the watercolor on the cover of this book, has her own gallery filled with beau-

Bernadette Chamberlain's art gallery.

tiful paintings of island life, as well as works by other artists, including American Sarah Honaker who spends part of the year on the island creating driftwood paintings.

Millicent Kelly, our local police deputy, also is an accomplished artist. Her work, along with other artists, is periodically featured in a corner of the yacht club dining room as well as the gift shop, where local art and books by this author are also for sale. Isles General and Lindsay's Boutique carry a selection of local artwork and books, as well as postcards and photography on canvas.

Joan Mann, who spends most of the year on the island, is perhaps our most famous artist, with works in several galleries in Nassau, Eleuthera and the States as well as on the island. Her paintings are in watercolor or acrylic and reflect daily life on the island, but she is also known for her colorful hand-painted t-shirts and fabrics, including the yacht club tablecloths, and most recently, custom tiles.

Gary Johnson, an American on South Staniel, has created outstanding watercolors that capture island life and village landmarks. His whimsical "This Way That Way" sign is a favorite photo op for visitors.

Old Stuff

Every island has its collectors and hoarders of "treasure," and Staniel Cay has a variety of interesting discards around the island: machinery that is now solid rust, boats that will never again float, airplane parts (and airplanes), old marine items and vehicles. I've included a few here, which may or may not be on the island in the future.

One of the hardest challenges of island life is discarding junk. Because it takes such an effort to get anything here, every little nut and bolt is tucked away for possible future use. If you can't find what you're looking for, it's not uncommon to ask around to see if someone else has it. Many times I've headed back to the States with items on my shopping list to replace what I borrowed. To some natives, however, "borrowing" can mean they are asking for a permanent gift. I don't think this old round engine will ever fly again, but you never know.

Hint...this propeller is NOT at the airport.

There are several pieces of old machinery around the island.

This vehicle is off the road for good.

This beauty is somewhere on South Staniel.

Bridge

Years ago, the only way to South Staniel was by boat or by land where the airport runway now sits. In the late 1970s, a bridge, primarily for walking, was built over the creek. As

The newest bridge, built in 2009.

more vehicles arrived on the island, the bridge underwent more stress and had to be rebuilt several times. The current bridge, strong enough to hold small trucks, was built in 2009, primarily by the residents of South Staniel. There is no fishing allowed from the bridge to protect the juvenile bonefish that live in the mangroves.

Mangroves

Staniel Cay is blessed with many mangrove trees, providing habitat for developing bonefish and many other marine species, while also securing sediment with the changing tides, protecting the area from erosion. The unique stilt root system is designed to keep salt water from the rest of the plant, and mangroves have developed ways of limiting the amount of water they lose through their leaves. While seeds of most trees

Mangroves hold tidal areas together.

germinate in soil, the seeds of the mangrove germinate while still attached to the parent tree. The seedling grows either within the fruit, or out from the fruit to form a propagule, capable of producing its own food through photosynthesis when it drops into the water. When it is ready to root, it floats vertically rather than horizontally in the water, enabling it to become lodged in the mud, where its roots take hold.

Century plant

This is a plant that occasionally produces a tall spike with big yellow flowers. When it does, the plant dies, producing suckers from the base to continue its growth. While it is called a century plant, the average life-span is around 28 years. The leaves can yield fibers, and in the early 1900s, these plants, along with sisal, were cultivated on Staniel Cay to produce hemp rope, which was exported to Nassau. After the 1926 hurricane, when much of the topsoil was washed from the island, many of the plants did not survive and labor intensive production of hemp stopped.

Century plant.

Village Almond Tree

At the main corner of the village in front of the Gray family home and across from the church and near the government dock, there is an area where the locals gather to play dominoes, eat their lunch, gossip or just to hang out. Some call it

Old almond tree in the Gray's yard.

the "love gathering tree." This ancient almond tree, with its gnarly trunk and shady canopy, was brought from Nassau about 90 years ago. And yes, it does produce almonds. The nearby genip and sapodilla fruit trees were planted at the same time.

Old Fire Hearth Chimney

The old stone cooker and oven, located near the water behind the church, dates from the mid to late 1800s. By the early 1900s, most homes had a separate cook house to keep the smoke and heat away from where people lived and slept. The cook hearth that stands today was actually the backside of a cookhouse. Legend has it that the owner, George Gib-

Cook hearth behind the church.

son, climbed into the hearth during the 1926 hurricane The cookhouse was destroyed, but his life was saved. Another hearth still stands at the Blue Store, where Burke Smith uses his old cook house for storage.

Because the island is blessed with such a pleasant climate

Burtke Smith's old cook house.

and most homes were very small, a lot of time was spent outdoors. Even today, visitors can see natives chatting on their covered porches or platting top to send to the straw merchants in Nassau via the mailboat.

Termite Nests

The chapter on termites describes the ongoing battle against these voracious pests, who seem to work around the clock destroying whatever wood is at hand. Long after a nest is poisoned, it still stands, and visitors can see many of them on the island. One of the oldest and largest dead nests is located off the north side of the footpath beyond the dump leading to the ocean ridge hiking trail. Since it's been dead for years, it's a good example of how well constructed and durable these mud homes are.

Termite nest on the path to the ocean hiking trail.

Staniel Cay Hiking Trail

The ocean park hiking trail at Staniel Cay was created in 2007 by members of the Staniel Cay Nature Conservancy. The views of the ocean beach and the rocky shoreline are spectacular. Rocks line the path, and at some points, little steps have been carved into the stone to make it easier to

The ocean park hiking trail is well marked and easy to walk.

There are interesting rock formations along the path.

Crinkly Rock Hill on the ocean trail.

Tropical storm waves batter the island off the trail.

walk. There are caves and craggy overhangs for exploring just off the trail, but be careful...it's a long way down. Toward the end of the trail, beware of pirates! Enjoy a swim off the beach before heading back to the village.

Picnic Beach

Staniel Cay's public beach is famous for its island cook-outs that may benefit a variety of organizations, individuals or causes: the children's annual school trip, sailing regattas, someone who may be very ill and need some financial help, the Staniel Cay Development Association, the annual library fundraiser and book sale held every Valentine's Day Satur-day, birthday parties etc. There is always a reason for a cook-

The public beach holds many picnics year round.

out to bring folks together, and it's one of the attractions for boaters to Staniel Cay. Many tenders and dinghys line the beach as they come from the anchorages to enjoy time ashore. It's also where the annual Staniel Cay New Year's Day Regatta trophy presentation and pig roast dinner are held.

Boat Yard

The boat yard, located off the main road between the air-port and church, usually boasts either *Lady Muriel* or *Tida*

Tida Wave undergoes a rebuild in the boat yard.

Wave undergoing refurbishing as our top Class A island sloops. It's also where the fleet of sunfish is stored for the junior sailors, where locals do repair work on small boats, and where some Class C racing boats are stored under cover.

A new boat ramp in the creek allows easy launching of boats on trailers.

The creek boat ramp allows launching of boats on trailers.

Wildlife
Birds

There is a wide variety of creatures in the Staniel Cay area, where its swimming pigs and endangered iguanas are a local tourist attraction.

There are many birds, from the majestic osprey, also known as a fish hawk, to the minute Bahama woodstar hummingbird. Ospreys can often be seen snatching fish from the sea or sitting in their giant nests.

An opsrey on Serenity's deck railing.

The Osprey is particularly well adapted to fishing, with reversible outer toes, sharp spicules on the underside of the toes, closable nostrils to keep out water during dives, and backwards-facing scales on the talons which act as barbs to help hold its catch.

Ospreys usually mate for life, and many nests are renovated each season, with some known to have been used for as many as 70 years. The nest is a large heap of sticks, driftwood and seaweed built in forks of trees, rocky outcrops, utility poles, artificial platforms or offshore islets. Be on the lookout, as there are several nests in the Central Exumas. If you get too close to one with chicks, as we did on, appropriately named Osprey Cay in the Exuma Land and Sea Park, you will be dive bombed by the parents until you leave.

The Bahama woodstar is the common hummingbird of the Bahamas, often seen near flowering trees and shrubs. It is an extremely tiny little bird, often mistaken for a large insect until you get a closer look.

Seagulls, often called the rats of the sea, appear from nowhere anytime there is food. Toss popcorn off Serenity's deck, and if it's gull season, they will swoop in for the take. We've thrown fish scraps in the air to have the seagulls grab them, then light on the boathouse roof for a leisurely feast.

The first of the three "Thunderball rocks" has a huge nesting population. On a quiet night, you can hear the birds calling to each other. Years ago, before the freight boat made regular trips to the island with fresh eggs, the villagers would

This curious bird is a frequent visitor, often hiding in the bush.

harvest the little bird eggs for food. There was a huge rebound in the bird numbers and varieties when this practice stopped. I'm not sure which birds nest on the island, but there are many varieties of terns and the little grey and yellow banana keets, as well as birds in the crane family.

Money Moth

Move something that's been sitting awhile, or open a door to a storage room or boathouse day or night, and it's almost certain you will see a money moth, or money bat as it's also called, the largest moth in the western hemisphere. Males can have a wing span as wide as sixteen inches, while the female reaches twelve inches.

In Jamaica and other places, the moth is seen as the embodiment of a lost soul, or a harbinger of bad things to come. In the Bahamas, it's the opposite. If a money moth lands on you, it's good luck! You can expect a windfall, and if it hits you in the face, even better. You just might win the lottery.

Crabs

Staniel Cay has a variety of crabs, from the humongous land crab that might be bigger than the bucket you put it in, to a variety of hermit crabs, both land and sea. The tiny ones don the little tree snail shells, while the larger soldier crabs that can pack quite a pinch, tend to like the black and white striped top shell. They are all scavengers, and will haunt any-place there is food. When I fed several feral cats in the past at Serenity, I had to make sure the food bowls were brought in at night, or the entire deck would be crawling with hundreds of soldier crabs. Very creepy.

One visitor expressed concern. If he got really drunk some night and didn't make it back to the cottage and passed out in the bush, would the crabs eat him? I smiled and didn't answer that one. Thankfully, he did not put it to the test.

Frogs
Serenity cottage is known for its chorus of froggers who live in and around the fresh water cistern. You can almost tell how much water is stored by the sound of their croaks. Many visitors have been surprised at how loud and consistent their chorus can be, never thinking it's a tiny little tree frog doing all that belching. They are an indication that the water is good.

Tree frog on Serenity's deck railing.

Lizards
There are so many varieties of lizards on Staniel Cay, from the bright green salamander to one with a long blue tail, that they have been the subject of an ongoing research grant from a university. For many years the researchers would come twice a year to monitor their habits, habitat and the effects of various controls, such as taking all vegetation off a small island rock to see how they survive, or keeping males in one enclosed pen and females in another. Supposedly they were monitoring all this to better humanity. If nothing else, it was

a good excuse for a vacation and we always looked forward to their return. Another researcher had a grant to study several varieties of Staniel Cay spiders. Any reason to visit is a good one.

The Famous Swimming Pigs

The swimming pigs of Big Majors Spot have been featured in many news articles and websites around the world. They are privately owned by a family on Staniel Cay, and have free run of the island, keeping company with a herd of goats that is rarely seen. One of the highlights of every visitor's vacation is to feed the pigs. As soon as they hear a boat approaching the beach (unless it's really hot and they've

A pig swims out to greet us at Big Majors Spot.

already gorged on donated scraps) they will swim out and expect a handout. Be careful. These are wild animals, and they have been known to take a knuckle or two, and will actually try to get in the boat if they think you are doling out the goodies too slowly. The faces change as new piggies are born and the older ones...well, you know how it goes. It's amazing to see the little piglets take to the water as if they are duck-lings. And it's hard to tell their squeals from those of children seeing the pigs for the first time.

Years ago, when Joe Hocher was talking to someone on Compass Cay, he was asked what kind of fish were caught in the area. He replied, "hog fish, grouper, pig fish..." The man interrupted him, saying he knew about hog fish and grouper, but he had never heard of a pig fish.

Without cracking a smile, Joe replied, "There's one now, swimming over from Pipe Cay," pointing to a feral pig. In those days, many of the islands had wild pigs, and natives often went hunting for boar.

Iguanas

The Exumas has its own species of iguanas that are totally protected. They are on various islands throughout the Exu-mas, but those on Bitter Guana and Gualin Cays are the sub-ject of ongoing research.

We helped catch, bag and tag the iguanas on one of the

An iguana at Bitter Guana Cay.

-236 -

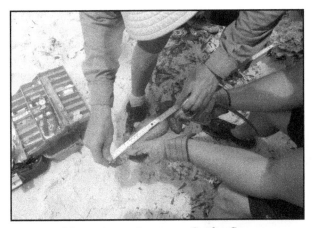

Measuring an iguana at Gaulin Cay.

Injecting a microchip into an iquana at Gaulin Cay.

researcher's visits to Gualin Cay. It was a hunt through the bush with two people corralling the iguanas while the third person caught them in a net. Each iguana was weighed, measured, and scanned for a microchip. If the iguana was already part of the study, data was updated and its number painted on with white-out so they wouldn't catch it again that trip. First-catch iquanas received a microchip injected beneath the skin and all data recorded.

We were told that the species in the Exumas is unique to the area and exist nowhere else. It's important that visitors do not feed them so they do not become dependent on handouts. The researchers emphasized that the reason they are thriving on the cays is due to the plentiful supply of seagrapes and other food. The last thing they want is for humans to disrupt their natural lifestyle.

Speaking Bahamian

Most visitors have a difficult time understanding some Bahamians, especially when the young men talk fast and loud, even if they are speaking a form of the King's English. Over the years it's been mixed with a little Jamaican, Creole, Indian, American English, as well as European languages to form their own dialect.

"Tingum" is a popular word, and can mean anything. Expressions "for true," "no problem, mon," "um-um-um" "baker" for oven, "mudda sick" (oh my God), "Don't make no mind to me, mon" and "reach" for "arrive" are some of the popular expressions. "Washing" refers to laundry, and if it's "on the chain" it means it's really good. They "go to the shop" instead of the store.

Bahamians usually skip the "h" in anything beginning with "th." A child is "tree" years old. Another peculiarity is the switching of "w's" and "v's, mostly at the beginning of a word:" "Vitch vay?" and "wowels." So, "wedding vows" may sound like "vedding wows."

Bahamian Food

Like most cultures, Bahamians have their own distinctive cuisine, with conch probably the most staple seafood. It's also said to contribute to large families, enhancing male potency, with the men believing "conch does gi'e man strong back." It can be eaten raw (conch salad is fabulous, with sour orange or lime naturally tenderizing the tough meat), fried, cracked, baked, stewed, or in a chowder...it is an extremely versatile food. In the old days, Bahamians would use a glass Coke bottle to pound the meat until tender, but nowadays a meat tenderizing tool or even a food processor is used. The harder it's beaten or "bruised," the more tender the conch.

Lobster, crab and many varieties of fish are also favorites, with a Bahamian "fish fry" comprised of whole fish, usually snapper, highly seasoned and then fried crisp – head, bones, eyes and all.

A favorite breakfast is tuna and grits. Holidays usually feature a whole roast pig, with ribs and chicken a favorite, accompanied by Bahamian style peas and rice and macaroni and cheese, the best I've ever eaten and what I miss most when I'm stateside.

Bread pudding, johnny cake and guava duff, a type of cake, are favorite desserts.

Souse is a popular one-dish meal which can have any kind of seafood, chicken, turkey, pig's feet or sheep tongue as a base. Whatever is handy – potatoes, onions, carrots, hot peppers, spices – gets thrown in the pot and boiled until done. It's a favorite on the weekend so food is readily available when anyone is hungry.

***

Of all the progress on the island, I would have to say that for me, internet availability is the single improvement that drastically changed my life. Up until that point, I could only visit the island on vacation, always wondering if I was missing a phone call or message. The internet allows me to live on the island year round without missing a beat. I am able to answer emails, handle vacation rentals, and be in touch with family members at a reasonable rate via internet phone.

No place is ever perfect. But, given all the ups and downs of Staniel Cay, it's a beautiful, inviting place to live, and certainly one of the best, if not THE best, island in the Bahamas to visit. Knowing it is what it is, as the natives say, makes it easier to look past the negatives, to lighten up on the frustrations of daily living, and to enjoy the moment. I just have to look out my window at the beautiful water and my gratitude for God's beauty is overwhelming. Paradise does have its price, but for me, it has definitely been worth it. When I go back to the States I am overwhelmed with traffic, rudeness, and lack of "community." When I return to Staniel Cay, I have a true sense of being home, that God's in his heaven and all's right with the world.

Staniel Cay – Then and Now

Aerial from the early 1970s.

Aerial taken in 2009.

About the Author

Martha (Marty) Crikelair Wohlford brings a wealth of knowledge and experience to her work.

She is a graduate of St. Mary's College, Notre Dame, Indiana, where she majored in English literature and creative writing.

Her novel, **Drumbeat No Lie**, has received favorable reviews, a "fun tale that makes for easy reading" set on a tiny Bahama island where drug smugglers invade a peaceful community.

She has written a work of nonfiction, ***If I Can't Be Dead, How Can I live?***, as well as two children's books.

Marty lives mostly at her home on Staniel Cay in the Bahamas, where she nourishes her spirit.

Internet: www.mwpr.com • email: marty@mwpr.com

CPSIA information can be obtained
at www.ICGtesting.com
Printed in the USA
FSHW021506010319
55957FS